3220 7598

ELEMENTS OF ARCHITECTURAL DESIGN

A PHOTOGRAPHIC SOURCEBOOK

SECOND EDITION

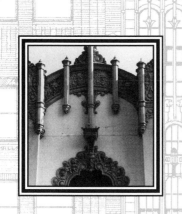

ERNEST BURDEN

John Wiley & Sons, Inc.

New York • Chichester • Weinheim • Brisbane • Singapore • Toronto

CIP DATA

This book is printed on acid-free paper. ∞

Copyright © 2000 by John Wiley & Sons. All rights reserved.

Published simultaneously in Canada.

This publication is designed to provide accurate and authoritative information in regard to the subject matter covered. It is sold with the understanding that the publisher is not engaged in rendering professional services. If professional advice or other expert assistance is required, the services of a competent professional person should be sought.

Library of Congress Cataloging-in-publication data:

Burden, Ernest E., 1934
    Elements of architectural design : a photographic sourcebook / Ernest Burden.-- 2nd ed.
      p. cm.
    Includes biographical references and index.
    ISBN 0-471-37117-3 (pbk. : alk. Paper)
    1. Architectural design. I. Title.

NA2750 .B864 2000
721--dc21

                         00-36840

Printed in the United States of America

10 9 8 7 6 5 4 3 2 1

1: STYLE

2: COMPOSITION

3: MATERIALS

4: COMPONENTS

5: FORM

ACKNOWLEDGMENTS

Oftentimes a major revision to a book, such as this one, presents more unforseen obstacles than producing the original edition. In this case, the challenge was matching the equipment and technology used for the original edition to arrive at a seamless blend of existing and new material.

I want to thank my editor, Margaret Cummins for initiating the book's revival, and her ongoing patient guidance through the production process. I also want to thank the entire production staff for making the quality of this edition exceed the original.

A very special thanks to Joy for her kind assistance, understanding and patience during the long design and production process.

This book examines the elements of architectural design throughout the ages, in particular those that exist in our own built environment. It has been designed so that each chapter is thematically related to the other chapters. Each presents a different aspect of design viewed from the standpoint of historical style, design vocabulary, building materials, components of buildings, and by its expression as architectural form.

The approach does not highlight any particular style or movement; rather, it presents all styles equally. It does not focus on the work of any one architect or architectural movement. The only commentary on any structure or component is to simply describe it as an object in our environment. Subjective evaluation or criticism about its success or failure is irrelevant to this work.

The aim is to underscore the importance of those buildings or styles that may have influenced successive structures. Needless to say, it is not possible to include every significant building ever built in the world over the last few thousand years. Therefore, this treatment is intended as an overview, and one that hopefully will stimulate the reader to search for more detail and to observe the built environment more keenly.

Buildings are identified by approximate periods only; addressing a specific history of architecture is not the purpose of this work. Many fine historical references are available to those who wish to research specific buildings or their architecture in more detail. It is important to understand the way early civilizations approached the use of materials, and how the various components evolved and developed over the ages, and to see the distinctive metamorphosis of architectural form.

The format of this book is to analyze the design of buildings within several interrelated chapters: style, composition, materials, components, and form. Except for the chapter on style, which is organized chronologically, the elements within each chapter are organized alphabetically. Building components are visually compared throughout the book as isolated elements, so the reader can examine the similarities that exist in all ages and in all styles.

We do not live in a vacuum, and we cannot design in one. The material in this book is offered as a stimulus to those who wish to discover new ways of looking at and interpreting more creatively the built environment.

A glance at the architecture of all past ages reveals to us that building is intimately connected with the fabric of life itself; economic, social, religious, and political. It is hard to imagine human existence without some form of shelter; the need for refuge is instinctive. It seems natural then that we build structures to meet that need. We are accustomed to thinking of buildings as the homes we live in, the offices and shops we work in, the places we worship, and the vast arenas for our recreation. Yet the majority of structures covering the earth offer more than shelter, more than refuge, and more than utility. That 'something more' is what we call architecture.

The history of architecture and the history of civilization are so closely intertwined that it is possible to understand early civilizations through their buildings and their art forms. Structures that have survived from the past can be considered "fossils of civilization," particularly valuable because the written records of many early cultures have perished. Monumental remains and stone carvings are the principal sources of information.

History plays an important role in helping us understand design in a larger sense - which is not to say we should copy the forms and attitudes of bygone periods; but we can create in relation to a much wider historical background. History is not simply the repository of facts and forms, but a process, a pattern of living and changing attitudes and interpretations. We find that when we study historical work in these relative terms that architects of previous eras were no less sensitive, no less talented, and no less intuitive than we are. We look backward to a past age not for a pattern that is the same for all ages, because each spectator in every period, at every moment, will inevitably transform the past according to his or her own experience.

How does one go about finding structures worth studying? Often, they are hidden by our familiarity with our own environment; our everyday routine may conceal their meaning. Ideally, all buildings should be visited in person, but this is physically impossible. Furthermore, there is information worth having that the eye alone cannot see. To comprehend a great cathedral or a modern complex, we need a schematic diagram on paper and probably a cross-section as well.

We can begin by looking at the environment as a collection of museum pieces, of manifested creativity. We must look up, as many buildings, especially older ones, are often different above the first floor. The way to understand the built environment is to look at all elements closely, inquisitively, and thoroughly, and to study these elements, not to lose ourselves or imitate the past, but to set higher goals for our own design achievement in the future.

Students of the Ecole des Beaux Arts were sent to Greece and Rome to study monuments, ruins, and temples and to make elaborate reconstructed drawings of them. These artistic and architectural efforts are magnificent in their own right, but they did little to develop the individual's understanding or ability to experiment on his or her own. Fortunately, there are myriad sources of inspiration available to us today, and it is possible to view nearly every notable structure on earth documented in numerous publications and on film and video.

The photographs in this book provide another way in which to examine buildings in detail; many were taken with a telephoto lens to isolate each component. They give a flavor of the unique architectural heritage to be claimed whenever people look at the structures around them. Certainly, some forms are more unique than others, or more ostensibly beautiful according to individual tastes. Some are more innovative, but all represent the life force we call architecture in their own individualistic way. We may not like all of them, but we can learn from all of them. It is up to the individual reader to make his or her own exploration and adapt it to his or her own approach in creating architectural design.

This book may contribute to the development of a freer use of lines, shapes, and forms, which encourage a familiarity with past creative thinking, expression, and experimentation. Architectural design must go beyond the state that prevails at the moment. To plan, we must know what has gone on in the past and intuit what is coming in the future, not so much to prophesize, but to make a positive creative statement that results from a universal outlook on the world.

A universal outlook is the backbone of this work. These elements of architectural design - style, composition, materials, components, and form - both emphasize the continuity of design throughout the ages and illustrate similarities of concept from early periods to today. It's only when we understand how our predecessors expressed their talent and vision in their buildings that we can create our own truly original architecture.

The history of architecture is a process of continuous evolution. The development of styles and classifications may be handy for reference and for remembering how one period relates to another, but it is only an expedient way to categorize work that exists as the result of myriad social, political, intellectual, and economic forces. Therefore, architectural styles, which seldom exist in a vacuum, are really gradual transitions or metamorphoses of elements from one civilization to the next.

There is a distinction between a building characterized by a certain style and a building having style. Every building that exists, for better or worse, has style. By that we mean the way in which something is done, as distinguished from its materials. A style can also be described as a gathering of forms used repeatedly on a number of buildings from a single historical period. When they are used over and over, they become characteristic of buildings of that period.

Styles either evolve from their predecessors or are evidence of a reaction against them. On a broader scale, there is no simple linear pattern of one style replacing another style. There are local variations within styles, and comparable developments have occurred at quite different times in different places. There are also instances where stylistic innovations have been adopted by cultures great distances apart. Although architectural styles may be discussed in chronological order, they often overlap, and more than one style exists at any given time.

Different styles influence one another and are modified as they mature or spread from their place of origin to other locations. Some styles are almost wholly derivative, freely borrowing from other styles; others, such as the revival styles, trace their origin more clearly back to a specific historic period. A few, such as the Modern Movement, are truly innovative, derived mostly from contemporary technology and materials. But technology and materials alone do not make a new style. A new style is born only when a single creative person adapts new building materials into new architectural forms.

Many styles rose from the ashes that consumed their predecessors, but many other contributing factors changed or caused a particular style to spread. In medieval times, construction usually stretched over a long period of time. It is not unusual to find Gothic cathedrals completed in a different but related style to that in which it was started. Other factors affecting style include the available technology, the materials and how they are used, and local building practices and ordinances in place at the time. Early structures show evidence of several building campaigns, either in a fairly consistent manner or in a variety of styles. Sometimes, the function of a building is changed, hence alterations are made in a style that contrasts with the original. Occasionally, ruined buildings have been used as part of new buildings, or elements from them have been incorporated into the new structures. Sometimes, as in Japan, traditional ancient buildings were reconstructed again and again in their original stylistic form.

Many structures fall into a category that is called "vernacular," or eclectic, built in a combination of styles and not according to any academic standard. Yet all have sprung from some common heritage. They became prototypes, if only because there are limited geometric forms and materials to build with. Many structures were built from pattern books that showed how to reproduce the popular styles of the day. In other cases, traditional building concepts passed from generation to generation of designers and builders. By adapting architectural idioms to accepted tastes, budgets, available materials, and building skills, these efforts produced hybrid styles outside the textbook vocabularies and often outside current national architectural fashions. Although such vernacular structures seldom contain all elements of a formal style, they often present sufficient clues to indicate a building's derivation from a particular style or styles. These indicators include scale, proportion, massing, shape, materials, textures and finishes.

Architecture is not exclusively an affair of styles and forms, nor is it determined only by external conditions. It has a life of its own; it finds new forms and expresses them in new styles and forgets them again - only to be rediscovered generations later in new interpretations. While there are some definite periods in history when exhibitions or "manifestos" proclaimed the beginning of a new movement or style, such as the Bauhaus, De Stijl, or Futurist movements, the reality is that styles exist simultaneously as they are developed and built around the world. An architecture may come into being by all sorts of external conditions, but once it appears, it becomes an organism in itself, with its own character, and its own continuing life - with its own style - and coexists with all the others.

What we have today, more than any other time in history, is a freedom from imposed style, almost an architecture without style. This can either be a curse or a gift to today's students and practitioners. Architecture can now reach out beyond the period of its conception, beyond the social and technical considerations that called it into being, and beyond the style from which it sprang, to become a truly original creation.

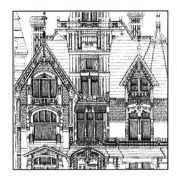

Style:
The way in which something is said or done, as distinguished from its substance. A sort; type, manner or method.
(from Latin stylus; writing instrument, style.)

When did style begin? The earth has been inhabited for more than a million years by human beings. For the majority of that period of time they were not concerned about a style or system of building. But they must have been concerned about shelter, which for the most part was there ready to use in the form of caves and other natural barriers. The caves became sanctuaries as well, as evidenced by their markings.

The caves at Lascaux, in France, dating back twenty millennia contain examples of artwork that shows both fear and reverence for the hostile natural environment. The inner sanctuaries of caves were reserved for ceremonies of life, death, and afterlife.

Since architecture can be described as the act of enclosing space for effective use, the early caves were a response to a wide variety of human needs. There are also examples of even earlier Stone Age huts. Most prehistoric settlements around the world occur around the sixth millennium B.C.

Some of the earliest records show other structures that have survived, such as megaliths, monuments, and tombs. Up-ended stones were the simplest form of megalithic structures. These were objects in open rather than enclosed space. They were used mainly as geographic or astrological reference points

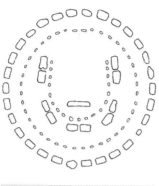

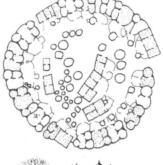

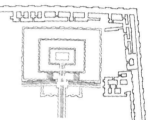

The tombs, in contrast, were made up of a boxlike chamber of slabs with a flat stone on top. As the structure rises above a certain height, the stones projected inward, narrowing the top. This was the earliest form of corbelling.

In Malta there is a temple complex from the third millennium B.C. In form it resembles Paleolithic caves, yet it is wholly man-made, thought-out and reproducible. As such it is the first true building type, an architectural form invented for a specific purpose.

The most famous of Neolithic monuments is Stonehenge. The early Britons who built and rebuilt it over a span of a thousand years appear to have used it as an astronomical observatory.

Early dwellings used reeds tied together in bundles, and these forms and methods were transferred into more permanent buildings. But once the problem of shelter was solved effort was devoted to communal life. The greatest achievements usually were works of sacred character, places of worship, or tombs and monumental architecture. The history of architectural styles then is the history of civilization written on clay tablets, in sun-dried bricks, in concrete, steel, glass, timber and stone.

By the year 3000 B.C. there were urban civilizations of considerable sophistication in three main areas: Egypt, Sumer, and the Indus valley. Early excavations have revealed large cities of mud-brick houses, with water supply and drainage, built on a grid system of streets. In Sumer there are remains of a number of ziggurats, vast stepped temples placed in large precincts, built mostly of mud-brick.

Sumerian (5000-2000 B.C.)

The architecture was made of locally available materials: clay tied bundles of reeds and were used as structural framing for huts and halls. Sundried bricks were used for the walls between the buttresses. Temples and palaces were built around a series of courtyards. The ziggurat of Ur is the most famous of the many that were constructed.

Mesopotamian (3000-500 B.C.)

Mud-bricks set with clay mortar made up this primarily massive architecture. The heavy walls were articulated by pilasters and recesses. Important public buildings were faced with glazed brick. Columns were seldom used, and openings were small.

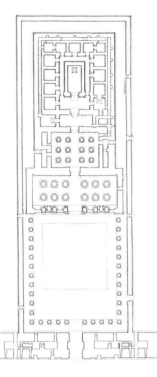

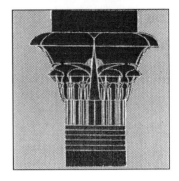

The earliest pyramids of Egypt are stepped like the temples in Sumer. The complex contains a wall enclosure, with the first stone columns with capitals. Columns are not yet free-standing, but they will soon become one of the most significant elements in building. The later columns were rather heavy and often elaborated with painting and carvings. There were many varieties of columns, and they were often used side by side. The capitals were distinctly ornate, with designs based on the lotus, papyrus, or palm.

Egyptian (3000 B.C.-200 A.D.)

The origins of Egyptian architecture can be traced to the reed huts and boat cabins of Neolithic times. The huts were built with inward sloping, or "battered" walls and thick bases to resist the annual inundation. This decorative, "bundling" of reeds later influenced stone construction, particularly fluted columns and capitals.

Egypt's notable achievements are its massive funerary monuments and temples built in stone for permanence, with post-and-lintel construction, corbel vaults without arches, and the pyramids. The style is characterized by massive walls and sturdy, close-spaced columns carrying stone lintels, which support a flat roof.

Courts and halls were designed to produce an impressive internal effect, and the hypostyle hall, crowded with columns, received light only from the clerestories above. Walls were carved in low relief. Colonnades and doorways were spanned by massive lintels in this trabeated architecture. Visually, Egyptian architecture is neither subtle nor sophisticated; the epic scale and drama provide the impact.

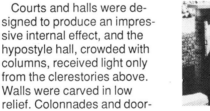

Ornament consisted of carvings rather than applied moldings, and the basis for the designs were either stylized figures or deities. The influence of Egypt, Persia and Mesopotamia on the architecture of Greece is easily traced.

Babylonian (2000-1600 B.C.)

An architecture characterized by mud-brick construction, had walls articulated by pilasters and recesses, sometimes faced with burnt and glazed brick. Elaborate palaces and temples have been unearthed. The city of Babylon contained the famous Tower of Babel and the Ishtar Gate, which was decorated with enameled brick friezes of bulls and lions.

It also contained the Hanging Gardens of Semiramis. Vast temple-terraces and artificial mountains were built in which astrologer priests consulted the heavens.

The ruins of the Assyrian Royal Palace of Khorsabad show a huge complex and remarkable for its monumental sculptural decoration. A more impressive site is the Palace of Darius located at Persepolis, with its magnificent relief carvings. Persepolis was destroyed in retaliation for the destruction of the Acropolis at Athens one hundred fifty years earlier by the Persians. Thereafter Greek architecture dominated the Middle East, while many Persian craftspeople went further east to work in India.

Minoan (1800-1300 B.C.)

A Bronze Age civilization flourished in Crete. Most important were its palaces. Gate buildings with multi-columnar porches provided access to unfortified compounds. Foundation walls, piers and lintels were stone with the upper walls in timber framework. Rubble masonry was faced with stucco and decorated with wall frescoes. Ceilings were of wood, as were the frequently used columns with simple balloon capitals and a downward tapering shape.

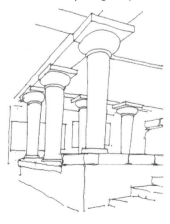

Mycenaean (1600-1200 B.C.)

The earliest phase was exemplified by masonry sidewalls and a timber roof. There were stone-faced, inclined access passages leading to the entrance with sloping jambs. There was a stone lintel supporting a characteristic triangular relief sculpture.

Indus Valley (1500-1200 B.C.)

There were a few cities that flourished in the Indus valley. They were carefully planned on a grid system, with main boulevards forming rectangular blocks. They were mostly of mud-brick construction.

Assyrian (900-700 B.C.)

Mesopotamia was conquered by the Assyrians, whose architecture was characterized by mud-brick buildings. Stone was used for carved monumental decorative sculptures. Excavations have uncovered large palaces and temple complexes with ziggurats as well as extensive fortifications.

External walls were plainly treated, but ornamented with carved relief sculpture or with polychrome bricks. Doorways were spanned by semicircular arches featuring glazed brick around the circumference. The windows were square headed and high up in the wall.

The interior courts were all large, and filled with columns. They were slender and widely spaced, as they only had to support timber and clay roofs, instead of slabs of stone. A most distinctive type of column was developed with a high molded base, fluted shaft and capital of recurring vertical scrolls. The bracket form of the topmost part was fashioned with the heads of twin bulls. This was similar to the development of the Ionic order taking place in Greece.

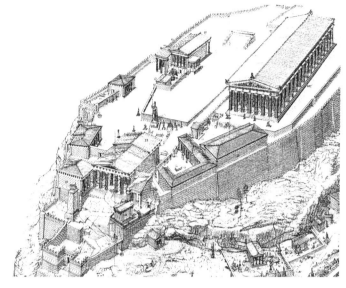

Greece (800-300 B.C.)

The architecture of Greece has been for some the source of the highest artistic inspiration, and has influenced all styles up to our own time. The first manifestation was a wooden structure of upright posts supporting beams and sloping rafters. The wood architecture was later reproduced in stone. The subtle artistic sense of the Greeks produced a delicacy of outline, perfected proportions and refined treatment.

The Greeks discovered the rules governing the harmony of form and sought to design with a sense of balance and proportion. There was an extreme conservativism of structural form due to the post-and beam construction. They set limits to the style, then refined the design before passing it on to succeeding generations. It was a "kit of parts" kind of architecture, characterized by austerity and free of ornate carvings. Greek ornament is refined in character and most all succeeding forms of architectural ornament has been based on the contours developed by this culture. The materials were limestone and marble and were prepared with the highest standards of masonry, complete with sophisticated optical corrections for perspective (entasis).

The most famous of Greek buildings is the Parthenon on the Acropolis at Athens, which incorporates a whole range of refinements to compensate for certain optical illusions, such as the diminution of perspective, the curving appearance of straight lines, and other corrections. This suggests that they were more concerned with perfection than originality. The Parthenon became the most copied structure in all of history.

The most widely used elements of European architecture are the decorative column orders that were an integral part of this style: the Doric, which is the simplest and sturdiest, the Ionic, which was more slender, and the Corinthian, which had a very elaborate capital.

One of the buildings on the Acropolis is the Erectheum, a temple which shows the most exquisite workmanship of any ancient building. Its most noticeable feature is the replacement of some of the columns with female figures.

Etruscan (700-280 B.C.)

This architecture flourished in western central Italy until the Roman conquest. Apart from underground tombs and city walls, it is largely lost, but the characteristic arch influenced later Roman construction methods. The examples that survive show forms that were rich in ornamentation.

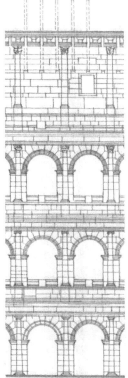

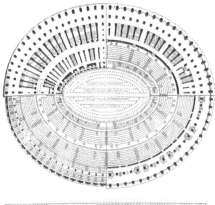

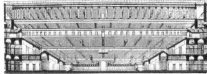

Roman (300 B.C.-365 A.D.)

The architecture of Rome was influenced by the Etruscans, and combined their use of the arch with the Greeks' columns. Rome itself offers the first real example of an urban architecture. It was far more adventuresome than the Greeks; although they worked within the classical orders, they were used with much more freedom. Greater attention was given to the development of other construction techniques. They were the first to create and manipulate large interior spaces. The invention and development of concrete led to a system of vaulting, which demonstrated their sophisticated engineering skills.

The building of ancient Rome placed an emphasis on monumental public buildings. It was generally regarded as an imposing scale, reflecting the grandeur of the empire. Buildings were large and very impressive. They were less concerned with form than the Greeks. They fully exploited construction possibilities using the arch and vault, and they developed the dome to roof a circular area. The vast monuments impress by their size and by their miraculous construction.

There was a deliberate separation of structure and decoration. The pilaster was used decoratively on walls instead of half-columns. Colonnades and arcades were both in use, and occur one above the other at times.

Elaborate ornamentation derived from the later Greek periods was used mainly on the interiors, while the exteriors remained austere. The Romans relied on the abundant carving on their moldings rather than on the contours. Ostentation replaced refinement. Marble, granite and alabaster were the primary facing materials, as well as stucco and mosaics.

Many of these building types had sophisticated building services, such as plumbing, heating and water supply. The Coloseum is probably the most impressive of these monuments. It could seat 50,000 spectators, and the arena could even be flooded for aquatic or naval displays.

On an urban scale it also produced an impressive array of planning elements. Formal axial planning with whole communities and towns constructed on a grid plan were typical. This urban architecture with its multiple building types strongly influenced the early Christian building styles.

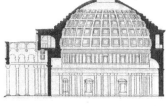

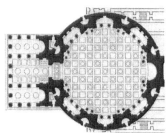

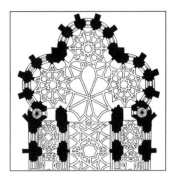

Medieval (400-1400)

This term is used to summarize the architecture of the European Middle Ages, in particular the Byzantine, Romanesque and Gothic, where it spanned a millennium. It was an age of the fortified castle, as feudalism grew to provide protection from invaders. Bishops' palaces rivalled cathedrals in splendor and, like castles, served public and private functions. As the population grew, smaller houses nestled around castle walls.

Indian/Buddhist
(300 B.C.- 320 A.D.)

In this originally timber and mud-brick architecture the earliest surviving buildings take three forms: living caves, rock-cut preaching caves, and stupas. These shrines were designed for large groups of worshippers. In the rock-cut temples, the main forms and details follow early wooden prototypes.

The stupa is a hemispherical mound with a processional path around the perimeter, with elaborately carved gateways. The most typical is the stupa at Sanchi.

The temples are elaborately carved stone shrines where the exterior is more important than the interior, and the entire building is a focus of worship. They also feature an exuberant and sensuous exterior covered with sculptural ornamentation.

Early Christian (200-1025)

The final phase of Roman architecture was found primarily in church building, and was related to the rise of the Byzantine style. The Roman basilica form was adopted as the ground plan for most early Christian churches. These simple rectangular plans, consisted of a nave with two side aisles, and a longitudinal and horizontal emphasis. Until the Renaissance, all cathedrals were based on these early Christian models.

Sassanian (200-600)

This architecture was prevalent in Persia, primarily in palace complexes. It featured extensive barrel vaults and parabolic domes set in plaster mortar. The massive walls were covered by pilasters and cornices. The most notable is the Palace at Ctesiphon.

Byzantine (300-1450)

A totally new direction was given to architecture when the seat of the Roman Empire moved to Byzantium; the new style became the official architecture of the church. It was certainly derived from the Romans, but differed from it in the arrangement of the plans and the general use of the dome or cupola. These plans were generally based on the Greek cross, with a large cupola rising from the center.

Arches were either semicircular or horseshoe. Capitals were tapered square blocks and they were highly ornamented. The style was further characterized by large pendentive supported domes, arches and elaborate columns, and richness in decorative elements.

Doorways were square-headed with a semicircular arch over the flat lintel. The round arch, segmented dome, and use of marble veneer are also characteristic of this style The most famous example is the Hagia Sophia in Istanbul.

Indigenous American
(500 B.C.-1500 A.D.)

The native American architectural styles range from the wigwams and longhouses of the Indians in the forested areas and teepees of the Plains Indians, to the igloos of the Eskimos. It also includes the sophisticated communal pueblo cities carved out of mountainsides or built out of adobe in the Southwest.

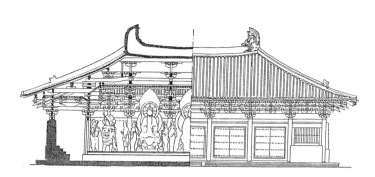

Chinese (400-1600)

Although the Chinese is one of the oldest civilizations known, very little evidence exists of the early forms of buildings. The records show that early wood structures with mud walls and thatched roofs were located in feudal cities designed on rectangular plans. There is also evidence of tombs built for aristocrats. Most early buildings were wood, with some use of other baked materials, such as bricks and tiles.

This highly homogeneous traditional architecture was repeated throughout the centuries. Stone and brick were used for permanent structures such as fortifications. Otherwise, structures were mostly wooden frameworks of columns and beams. The most prominent feature was the tile covered gabled roof, with widely overhanging eaves and upward curving eaves resting on multiple brackets. Pagodas had each floor articulated in a distinct rhythmical, horizontal effect.

In large temple structures, the podiums are of marble with ornamental balustrades. There are long horizontal roofs of tile with upturned eaves. The general style uses post-and-beam construction based on modular rectangular bays, and large curved roofs supported on intricately carved timber brackets and beams. The timber trusses allowed multiple roof shapes. Palace design became elaborate with heavy ornamentation, but naturalistic features such as gardens and courts were very important functionally and philosophically.

Japanese (500-1700)

Strongly influenced by Chinese design, this architecture was based exclusively on timber construction. Simple pavilion structures consist of a wooden framework of uprights and tie beams supported by a platform. Nonbearing walls are constructed of plaster and wood with sliding partitions. Doors and windows are lightweight material. The tiled hipped roofs project wide overhangs with upturned eaves as the result of elaborate bracket systems. Stone is used only for bases, platforms, and fortification walls.

Great emphasis is placed on the integration of buildings with their surroundings, with open verandas providing the transition. The style has a unique vitality and abstract purity. A high standard of carpentry evolved and provided a rich source of inspiration for many modern architects in terms of siting, composition, and construction.

A formal axial planning was used for most major temples, while domestic buildings were less formal. Light translucent screens divide interior spaces with a simplicity of design and skillful balance of decoration and plain material. There is a strict modular approach to layout, which is based on the tatami mat and governs the entire design of the house. There is an extremely conservative approach to construction, and carpenters became skilled in designing individual types of joints.

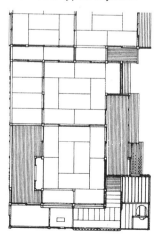

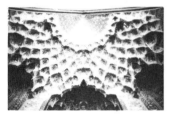

Moorish (500-900)

This style was prevalent in Spain and Morocco, but was somewhat isolated from the major developments elsewhere. The influences were Mesopotamian brick and stucco techniques. There was frequent use of the horseshoe arch. Many Moorish buildings made use of Roman columns and capitals. Vaults developed into highly complex and ornate forms.

Brick was the major material, used both decoratively and structurally in combination with marble. Stone was used for decoration by contrasting it with brick. The columns were limestone and marble with extensive use of stucco to build up the richly molded surfaces, which were painted with bright colors and sometimes even gilded.

Iranian (500-1000)

This style had an immense effect on Islamic architecture. This is particularly true of the decorative treatment of patterned brickwork, colored tile and molded stucco. Other attributes are the use of stalactite vaults. The essential elements are richly decorated surfaces, brightly colored tiles and molded stucco. The minaret was evolving into a star form that had an influence on Indian architecture.

Islamic (600-1500)

Mesopotamia and Graeco-Roman are the two main sources for this style. The mosque was a major outlet for artistic design and craftsmanship. It makes use of symbolic geometry, using pure forms such as the circle and square. The major sources of decorative design are foliage, geometric shapes and Arabic calligraphy.

The major building types are the mosque and the palace. Plans of the mosque are based on a rectangular courtyard with a prayer hall. The layouts are strongly symmetrical; forms are repetitive and geometrical. The surfaces are richly decorated with glazed tiles, carved stucco and patterned brickwork or bands of colored stonework.

India / Hindu (600-1750)

All types of temples in this style consist of a small unlit shrine crowned by a spire and preceded by one or more porch-like halls, used for religious dancing and music. These temples are the very opposite of the Greek temple. Hindu sculptors carved every element as unique, and used repetition to achieve a unifying context.

There was no attempt to evolve a style, or perfect a pillar or column. Even without color the wealth of detail and the sensual portrayal of human forms that adorn every surface is without equal. The stone was laid rough-cut and carved in place.

Meso-America (1300-500 B.C.)

There is a widespread incidence of monumental architecture in all early civilizations. This is especially striking in the great temples and pyramids of Pre-Columbian America, which are equivalent to those of ancient Egypt and the Middle East. The main centers are in Mexico and Peru, which are divided into four main cultures: Mayan, Toltec, Aztec, and Inca. All four civilizations conceived of their architecture in monumental terms characterized by strong grid plans, huge walled enclosures, and vast stone cities.

Mexican buildings were noted for funerary architecture, large underground tombs entered by stairs, and decorated with friezes and wall paintings. One of the most notable sites is Monte Alban, a carefully planned ceremonial complex.

Recent excavations have shown that many of the early temples were covered over with later buildings, sometimes as many as three layers deep. The inner surfaces are thus preserved to show early surface color and decoration.

Mayan (600-900)

Sites such as Tikal in Guatemala, Copan in Honduras, and Palenque represent the highest development of this style. It is characterized by a monumental construction that includes soaring temple pyramids, palaces with sculptural facades, ritual ball courts, plazas and interconnecting quadrangles. Buildings were erected on platforms, often with a roof structure.

Decorative elements formed open parapets. The interior walls were massive. The lower section was a continuous frieze carrying intricate decoration of masks, human figures, and geometric forms. Exterior surfaces of structures, were covered with a lime stucco and were painted in bright colors.

The sites were totally rebuilt periodically, leaving previous structures completely covered and intact. One of the most notable examples is Chichen Itza in Yucatan, the site of the largest center of the Mayan civilization.

Zapotec (700-900)

This eclectic architecture is found in Oaxaca, Mexico. The Zapotecs assimilated influences from the Olmecs (700-300 BC) and especially from Teotihuacan (300 - 900 AD). It culminated in a recognizable regional style, characterized by pyramids having several stepped terraces. These were accented with balustrades whose tops were decorated.

Miztec (700-1000)

In Oaxaca, Mexico a type of architecture developed which was characterized by great mass, use of interior stone columns, and emphasis on horizontal lines. The minutely detailed fretwork of the interior and exterior paneled friezes was produced by an assembly of thousands of small decorative elements set into clay. There was some Zapotec influence. At Mitla there are free-standing buildings around large courts, which were oriented towards the cardinal points of the compass.

Toltec (800-1200)

An austere geometric architecture formed the basis for the Aztec style and others. It was characterized by the use of colonnades, square carved roof supports, monumental serpent columns, and narrative relief panels set in plain wall surfaces. Tula was one of the major sites representing this style.

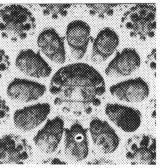

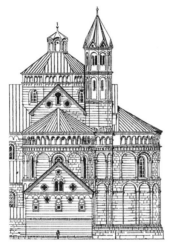

Gothic (1050-1530)

A revolutionary style of construction of the High Middle Ages in western Europe was emerging from Romanesque and Byzantine forms. The term "Gothic" was originally applied as one of reproach and contempt, although the style was very popular and spread rapidly.

It was primarily characterized by a delicate balance of forces, with the thrusts directed throughout a rigid structural lattice. It was most often found in cathedrals employing the rib vault, pointed arches, flying buttresses and the gradual reduction of the walls to a system of richly decorated fenestration.

Its features were height and light, achieved through a mixture of skeletal structures and ever increasing windows. One of the finest and oldest French Gothic example, Notre Dame, clearly shows the elements. Fine-grained limestone made it possible to accurately fit the members and moldings. Walls were no longer necessary to support the roof and could be replaced with huge windows of stained glass.

Romanesque (800-1180)

The style emerged from Roman and Byzantine elements, characterized by massive articulated wall structures, arches and powerful vaults. It lasted until the beginning of the Gothic period.

It reached one of its most refined forms in Tuscany, and arcades with semi-circular arches and geometrical facades were called Proto-Renaissance. It was also the precursor of the Gothic style. It showed an evolution of stone vaulting, and of the rib method of construction. There was a visual and conceptual unity of design in the plan and use of the major and minor spaces, structure and ornamentation.

It was characterized by heavy masonry construction, sparse ornament, plain walls, with decoration derived from the structure. It also featured thick molded piers, assembled from small stones individually carved to fit. Smooth surfaces prevailed.

Anglo Saxon (800-1066)

The pre-Romanesque architecture of England before the Norman period is represented by this style. It survived for a short time thereafter, and was characterized by its massive walls and round arches.

Norman (1066-1180)

A Romanesque form of architecture predominated in England from the Norman Conquest to the rise of the Gothic. In the early stages it was plain and massive, with few moldings confined to small features. Archways were plain and capitals were devoid of any ornament. As the style advanced, greater enrichment was introduced, and later examples exhibit a profusion of ornament. Windows resemble small doors without mullions. Pillars were slender and channelled.

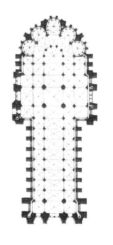

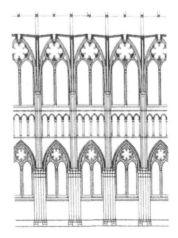

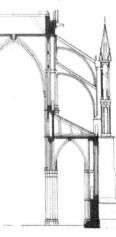

Aztec (1100-1520)

All Pre-Columbian civilizations conceived of their architecture in monumental terms. They left a legacy of pyramidal forms, huge wall enclosures, and vast stone cities, used primarily for festivals.

Aztec architecture emerged from the austere forms of the Toltecs. It was characterized by strong grid plans, monumental scale, brightly colored exteriors, often with highly stylized surface carvings of human figures, floral patterns and their gods. Their pyramids often supported two temples with parallel stairways. Destruction by the Spanish left few remains, as the Aztec capital of Tenochtitlan is entirely buried under modern Mexico City.

Chimu (1150-1400)

A style dominant in northern Peru featured houses that were built in rows along symmetrically laid out streets inside high city walls. Buildings were constructed of adobe with wooden lintels. Walls were decorated with wide moldings with geometrical designs.

Inca (1200-1500)

The last of the Pre-Columbian cultures was that of the Incas, whose empire lasted until the fifteenth century. Their building was characterized by its megalithic masonry. This is exemplified in the ceremonial buildings of the mountain city Machu Picchu. This was the last fortress to resist the Spanish invaders.

India / Hindu-Buddhist (1113-1150)

Hindu and Buddhist religion had a strong influence on Far East temple architecture. One of the most well-known sites is Angkor Wat, a temple complex of shrines intended as a funerary monument in Cambodia. It is perhaps one of the world's largest religious structure and was conceived as a "temple mountain."

It is within an enormous enclosure and surrounded by a wide moat. It is approached by a monumental causeway formed by giant mythical serpents leading to the entrance gate. The temple is built on a series of stepped terraces, surrounded by towers at each corner. Vaulted galleries receive light from an open colonnade illuminating the continuous relief friezes, which adorn the inner walls. The central sanctuary is a large pagoda-like tower on top of a stepped pyramid. It is joined by passageways to towers at each of the four corners of the base.

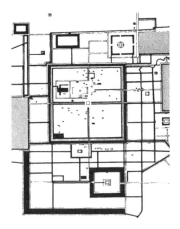

Early English (1200-1250)

The first Gothic style to follow the Norman style featured molding, consisting of rounds and deep hollows, which produced a strong effect of light and shadow. The arches were lancet shaped and pointed.

Doorways were generally very deeply recessed with numerous moldings in the arch and jambs, which are nearly always detached from the wall. Windows are long and narrow, and almost always pointed. Pillars consist of small shafts arranged around a larger central pier.

Villard de Honnecourt (c. 1235)

French architect whose notebook is an invaluable source of information on thirteenth-century building materials.

Giotto di Bondone (c. 1266-1337)

Designed the Florence Cathedral campanile (1334), which combines Romanesque, Classical, and Gothic elements.

Decorated Style (1280-1350)

The second of the three phases of English Gothic was characterized by rich decoration and tracery and by the use of multiple ribs in the vaulting. The early development was very geometric, while the later forms were curvilinear, with complicated rib vaulting and naturalistic carved foliage.

Filippo Brunelleschi (1337-1446)

Florence-born architect who designed the dome of the Florence Cathedral; the Foundling Hospital, Florence (1421); St. Lorenzo, Florence (1425); and St. Spirito, Florence (1436).

Perpendicular (1350-1550)

The last and longest phase of Gothic architecture in England was characterized by a vertical emphasis and elaborate fan vaults. The final development is often referred to as Tudor style.

Thailand (1350-1500)

The most characteristic form of these temples is the eaves of the overlapping roof planes which are terminated with sculptural finials. The Temple of the Emerald Buddha in Bangkok is the most notable.

Renaissance (1420-1550)

The style developed during the rebirth of classical art and learning in Europe, followed Gothic as the dominant style, and then evolved through several periods into classicism. It was initially characterized by the use of the classical orders, round arches and symmetrical proportions.

It represented a return to the models of Graeco-Roman antiquity and the first instance of searching the past for inspiration. The degree of dependency on classical types varied throughout the period. It provoked great changes in both the church and secular buildings, and probably had more of an effect on architecture than any other period in history. Renaissance architects established a series of models of proportion and harmony which are still regarded as applicable. The early period in Florence is characterized by massive, rusticated palaces, sparsely decorated and fortress-like. A more adorned and fantastic architecture is found in Rome.

The building materials and methods continued in a direct line from the medieval. Even though there was a wealth of materials, many early Roman buildings were plundered for their stone. Architects took the new forms to France and eventually they spread to all of Europe. .

Pure Renaissance architecture was based on regular order, symmetry, and a central axis, with grandiose plans and impressive facades. Silhouettes were clean and simple, with flat roofs replacing Gothic spires. Walls of large dressed masonry blocks gave buildings an imposing sense of dignity and strength. The Gothic verticality was replaced with an emphasis on horizontality.

Semicircular arches appeared over doors and windows and in free-standing arcades. Columns were used decoratively on facades, and structurally in porticos. Ornamentation was based on pagan or classical mythological subjects.

Donato Bramante
(1444-1514)
High Renaissance architect, based in Milan, Italy. Designed the Tempietro of St. Pietro.

Michaelangelo Buonarroti
(1475-1564)
Architect, sculptor, painter and poet, who represents the Italian Renaissance at its height. In 1546, he was appointed architect of St. Peters, Rome.

Baldassare Peruzzi
(1481-1536)
Designed the Villa Farnesina, Rome (1505). Inside are brilliant frescoes by Raphael, Peruzzi, and others.

Raphael (Raffaello) Sanzio
(1483-1520)
High Renaissance architect and painter of great distinction. After Bramante's death, he was appointed master of works of St. Peters, Rome, and proposed a basilican version of Bramante's plan.

Antonio de Sangallo
(1485-1546)
Designed the Palazzo Farnese, the largest in Rome, and one of the most magnificent Renaissance palaces.

Leon Battista Alberti
(1404-1472)
Designed the marble façade of San Maria Novella, Florence, which contains classical details in an otherwise Gothic church. From Vitruvius, via Alberti, came the concept that buildings should be in proportion to the human body, and all their dimensions related. In 1452, wrote *De re Aedificatoria*, the first architectural treatise of the Renaissance.

Leonardo da Vinci
(1452-1519)
He built nothing, but produced a number of influential architectural schemes and designs.

Giacomo Barozzi deVignola
(1507-1573)
Born in Vignola, Italy, he became a leading architect in Rome following Michaelangelo's death. He wrote the *Rules for the Five Orders of Architecture* in 1562.

Andrea Palladio
(1508-1580)
St. Giorgio Maggiore and Il Rendentore are his two notable buildings in Venice (1566). His Villa Capra Vicenza (1567) is the most symmetrical of his villas, with porticoes on each side. His *Four Books on Architecture* was published in 1570.

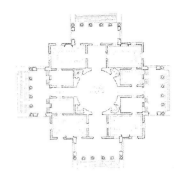

Palladianism (1508-1580)
Andrea Palladio was a Renaissance Italian architect whose *Four Books Of Architecture* set out in detail the classic orders, establishing in each one the proportions between the various components. He studied the Roman architect Vitruvius, and was fascinated by Roman symmetrical planning and the laws of harmonic proportions. His villas were the inspiration for much of the later country house building.

Pierre Lescot
(1510-1578)
One of the French architects who rebuilt the Louvre, Paris.

Mannerism (1530-1600)
The predominant style of this period of Italian architecture was a reaction against the classical perfection of the High Renaissance. It either responded with a rigorous application of classical rules and motifs, or flaunted classical convention, in terms of shape and scale. It was a more relaxed nonconformist style, and Baroque was its natural ultimate outcome, using unnatural proportion and willful stylistic contradictions.

Giorgio Vasari
(1511-1574)
The Uffizi Palace is his only significant work, and is Mannerist in style.

Carlo Maderna
(1556-1679)
Designed St. Susannah façade, Rome, a Baroque elevation crowded with orders, and set with niches rather than windows.

Elizabethan   (1558-1603)
The transitional style between the Gothic and Renaissance in England was named after the queen. It consisted mostly of designs for country houses, characterized by large windows.

Inigo Jones
(1573-1632)
London-born Royal Architect who introduced the Palladian style to Jacobean England and started the first Palladian revival. He worked on Old St. Paul's Cathedral, London, adding classical elements showing the power and scale of Roman architecture, which paved the way for Sir Christopher Wren when he began rebuilding the cathedral.

Pompeii
(1592)
The date that ruins of the city that was buried by the eruption of a volcano in 79 AD were first discovered. Excavations did not begin until 1709.

Baldassare Longhena
(1595-1682)
Designed St. Maria della Salute, Venice, sited at the head of the Grand Canal. It is the architect's masterpiece.

Gianlorenzo Bernini
(1598-1680)
Designed St. Peter's Piazza, the Vatican, and Colonnade, a huge elliptical space surrounded by a colonnade with columns four deep (1656).

Francesco Borromini
(1599-1677)
Highly original Baroque architect who rivaled Bernini. He designed San Carlo Alle Quattro Fontane, Rome, a church in which convex and concave wall surfaces are juxtaposed both on the façade and on the interior.

Baroque   (1600-1760)
The Renaissance was replaced by the more ornate Baroque period, which grafted new forms onto the Classical and Gothic features. In Spain the influence of the Muslims was incorporated. In England the Renaissance later came under the classical influence until the development of Georgian, Regency and other refinements. America, not yet colonized, absorbed the style by way of English Palladianism, or the Georgian facades which reflect the style of symmetry and grandeur.

Baroque (1600-1760)

The French word meaning bizarre, fantastic or irregular was used to describe this new style. It was deliberate in its attempt to impress, and was the most lavish of all styles, both in its use of materials and in the effects it achieves.

The style relied very heavily on individual talent rather than perceived rules. There are therefore considerable variations in the execution of Baroque buildings. Mannerist styles were often adopted and carried to the extreme. It was bold, opulent and impressive, and it was distorted intentionally. Pediments are broken, and open facades undulate, while interiors are theatrical.

Claude Perrault
(1613-1688)

French architect, one of the designers of the Louvre, Paris.

Ali Mardan Khan
(1630-1653)

His design for the Taj Mahal is the best known Islamic tomb monument.

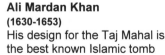

Sir Christopher Wren
(1632-1723)

A scientist and architect active in rebuilding London after the fire of 1666. He rebuilt St. Paul's Cathedral, London.

Louis XIV - XVI (1643-1792)

This high classical style was typified in the architecture, decoration and furniture of France, culminating in the building of Versailles. It developed into the Rococo style.

Jules Hardouin-Mansart
(1646-1708)

Designed the Church of the Invalides, Paris, the most Baroque of Parisian churches, with a dome derived from St. Peter's, Rome.

Colonial (1650-1700)

Architecture that is transplanted from the motherland to overseas colonies is classified as Colonial. Some examples are Portugese colonial in Brazil, Dutch colonial in New York, and English Georgian in the North American colonies.

The English brought provincial building techniques of wood framing and wood siding with steeply sloped roofs to America. The two-story front pitched down to a one-story rear, and was originally called the "saltbox," eventually becoming a formal style.

The Dutch were especially noteworthy in the manufacture and laying of brick and stone. The characteristic structural framing made the gambrel or double-pitched roof characteristic of the Dutch style.

The French settled in New Orleans and designed plantations often combining raised upper floors and roofs which projected over a veranda that was supported by ornate cast iron open grillwork columns.

Guiseppe Bibiena
(1657-1748)
Member of an important family of Italian painters, theatrical designers, and architects.

Jacob Prandtauer
(1660-1726)
Rebuilt Melk Abbey in 1702, which is dramatically sited above the Danube River; its façade is undulating Baroque.

Daniel Poppelmann
(1662-1736)
Designed the Zwinger Palace, Dresden, Germany, with Marcus Dietze. It is a Baroque structure with rich sculptural decoration.

Ecole des Beaux Arts
(1671)
The Parisian school goes back to its founding by the French architect Colbert, and became the most influential school of art and architecture in the 19th century. The Grand Prix de Rome, awarded by the school, provided several years of study at the French Academy in Rome. Many architects have been trained here; in practice, the school has been opposed to modern trends in architecture.

Francesco de Sanctis
(1693-1740)
Designed the Spanish Steps in Rome, along with Alessandro Specchi, which consist of an elegant ensemble of the piazza, the triple set of steps, and Bernini's fountain.

Giovanni Battista Piranesi
(1720-1778)
Published *Della Magnificenza ed Architecttura dei Romani*, and *Invenzioni Capric di Carceri,* the "Prisons" (c.1745).

Georgian (1700-1776)
A formal arrangement of parts within a symmetrical composition, enriched with classical detail characterize this style. The simple facade is often emphasized by a projecting pediment with colossal pilasters and a Palladian window. It often includes dormers, and the entrances are ornately decorated with transoms or fanlights over the doors. The style was transmitted through trade and architectural pattern books. It emphasized the orders, proportion, rules of taste and dignity, but in a modified and refined form. Georgian homes were built throughout early colonial America, and on many southern plantations.

Etienne-Louis Boulle`
(1728-1799)
His designs were extreme reactions against the Baroque style, and stressed plain shapes of enormous size without softening.

John Wood
(1704-1754)
Planned Bath, England, in the form of a Palladian-style Roman city, using crescent-shaped terraces.

Robert Adams
(1728-1792)
His work returned to the classical forms of antiquity, not their Renaissance-derived imitations. Adams excelled in using the natural early classical forms in domestic settings.

Claude-Nicholas Ledoux
(1736-1806)
His Neo-classical buildings combined simple shapes and austere treatments.

Thomas Jefferson
(1743-1826)
Designed Monticello, Virginia, his own house, in 1769.

Rococo (1750-1790)
A style of architecture and decoration, primarily French in origin, represened the final phase of the Baroque. It was characterized by a profuse, semi-abstract ornamentation. It was associated with lightness, swirling forms, flowing lines, ornate stucco work, and arabesque ornament, and It blended the separate members into a single molded volume.

Greek Revival (1750-1860)
The Greek contribution to Neo-Classical architecture stood for a purity and simplicity of structure and form. The buildings are square or rectangular. The proportions are broad, details are simple, facades are symmetrical and silhouettes are bold. There are free-standing columns supporting a pedimented gable. Many government and civic buildings are in this style.

Industrial Revolution
(1750-1890)
The evolution of this style was based on the production of iron and steel in quantities that colud be used as a primary building material. The very first iron frame structures were the industrial buildings, which evolved into the steel frame skyscrapers of modern times. The few pioneers of this new era were engineers and not architects.

Neo-Classicism (1750-1880)
The last phase of European classicism was characterized by monumentality, strict use of the orders, and sparing application of ornament. It was based on a more rational approach to design and a more correct archaeological interpretation of the earliest Graeco-Roman forms. In the extreme it was abstract in the use of volumetric space and the balance of simple shapes and masses.

John Nash
(1753-1835)
Planned Regent Park and Regent Street, London, as a picturesque scheme. He also designed the Brighton Pavilion for the Prince of Wales in a mixture of Indian, Chinese, and Gothic styles.

Sir John Soane
(1753-1837)
Designed Number 3 Lincoln's Inn Fields, London.

Pierre Charles L'Enfant
(1754-1825)
Designed a city plan for Washington, DC.

Charles Bullfinch
(1763-1844)
Architect of Boston churches and the Massachusetts State House (1795), a combination of Palladian and pure Classicism styles.

Benjamin Latrobe
(1764-1820)
Trained in Europe, but emigrated to the United States, where he met George Washington, and built a number of public buildings, including work on the Capitol; advised Thomas Jefferson on the design of the University of Virginia campus (1817).

Federal (1780-1820)
Low pitched roofs, a smooth facade and large glass areas characterize this style. Geometric forms accentuate the rhythm of the exterior wall. It is elegant and intentionally austere. Although it rejected the Georgian decoration, it retained its symmetry and the pilaster-framed entrance, fanlight and sidelights. Windows were simply framed and the quoins were abandoned.

Karl Friedrich von Schinkel
(1781-1841)
German architect of original Neo-classical buildings. His work was stylistically eclectic, but lyrical and logical. Schinkel's funeral in 1841 was a national event, his grave marked by a stele of his own design. King Friedrich Wilhelm IV (reigned 1840-1861) decreed that all Schinkel's work be purchased by the state.

Robert Mills
(1781-1855)
Designed the Washington Monument, the tallest obelisk that epitomized the romantic Classical ideals.

William Strickland
(1788-1854)
American architect, a pupil of Latrobe. He designed mostly in the Greek Revival style, as well as the Egyptian Revival style.

John Haviland
(1792-1852)
English-born American architect who designed in a severe Greek Revival style and later incorporated Egyptian Revivalist elements. He became know as the greatest Egyptian Revivalist.

Carpenter Gothic (1800-1880)

The application of Gothic motifs, often elaborate, by artisan builders in wood.

Pierre Henri Labrouste
(1801-1875)

A French architect whose reputation rests on the Bibliotheque Ste-Genevieve, Paris (1838) in which an iron structure was slotted into a masonry cage. The reading room of the Bibliotheque Nationale, Paris, employed the same exposed iron and glass interior (1854).

Sir Joseph Paxton
(1801-1865)

Designed the Crystal Palace, London, the first prefabricated building in iron, glass, and laminated wood.

Richard Upjohn
(1802-1878)

English-born American architect remembered primarily as a church architect and as a Gothic Revivalist. His most well-known building is Trinity Church, New York (1841). He was the first president of the American Institute of Architects, which he helped to found.

Paul Abadie
(1812-1889)

Designed Sacre-Coeur Church in Paris, and is best known for French Neo-Romanesque churches.

E. Emmanuel Viollet-Le-Duc
(1814-1879)

Architect and medievalist who was appointed to head the Ecole des Beaux-Arts in 1863. He wrote a *Dictionary of Architecture* in 1854.

Alexander Thomson
(1817-1875)

Scots Neoclassical architect, an original designer influenced by Schinkel, who worked mostly in Glascow. His buildings drew on a variety of sources, including ancient Egyptian, Persian, and even Indian architecture.

James Fenwick
(1818-1895)

Designed St. Patrick's Cathedral, New York City, a vast Gothic church.

John Ruskin
(1819-1900)

Wrote the *Seven Lamps of Architecture*, an influential book advocating functional planning and honesty in the use of materials in construction.

Frederick Law Olmsted
(1822-1903)

One of the most important landscape architects of the time, and an innovator in the design of public parks, much influenced by John Paxton's work in England. He designed Prospect Park in Brooklyn, and Central Park in New York City. His last large scheme was the World's Columbian Exposition, Chicago (1893), where he created a sylvan setting for the Neo-classical buildings of McKim, Mead & White, Daniel Burnham, and others.

Charles Garnier
(1825-1898)

Developed the luxury flat style in the rebuilding of Paris. He also designed the Opera House, the most showy Neo-Baroque building in Paris.

Richard Morris Hunt
(1827-1895)

Trained in France, he produced buildings in the United States in a variety of styles, mainly grandiose pastiche, for millionaire clients.

Guiseppe Mengoni
(1829-1877)

Designer of the Galleria Vittorio Emanuelle, Milan, Italy, the largest shopping arcade of its type in Europe.

Gingerbread (1830-1880)

A richly decorated American building fashion, particularly in the Victorian style.

George von Dollman
(1830-1895)

Designed Schoss Linderhoff, one of several palaces for Ludwig II of Bavaria, in an extravagant Neo-Rococo style.

Gustave Eiffel
(1832-1923)
Designed the Eiffel Tower, Paris. It was built of exposed steel for the 1887 Paris Exhibition, and for 40 years was the tallest structure in the world.

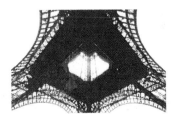

William Lee Baron Jenney
(1832-1907)
Studied in Paris, and set up an office in Chicago, Illinois. He was the first to use structural steel in a building for columns and girders. They were prototype skyscrapers. He taught Sullivan, Holabird, Roche, and Burnham in the problems of tall buildings.

Henry Hobson Richardson
(1838-1886)
Renowned for massive Romanesque buildings. He designed Trinity Church, Boston (1877), inspired by French and Spanish Romanesque styles.

Frank Furness
(1839-1912)
Designed the Provident Life and Trust Company, Philadelphia, in the high Victorian Gothic style, and designed the Academy of Fine Arts, also in Philadelphia. Louis Sullivan worked in his office before moving to Chicago.

Italianate (1840-1880)
This style is typified by a rectangular two or three-story house with wide eaves supported by large brackets, tall, thin first-floor windows, and a low pitched roof topped with a cupola. There are many pronounced moldings, details and rusticated quoins. The earmarks of the style are the arched windows with decorative "eyebrows" and recessed entryways. This style appeared in nearly every American city, large or small.

Gothic Revival (1830-1880)
This romantic style is distinguished by vertically pointed arches and steep, complex gable roofs with finials and medieval decorative motifs.

Romanesque Revival
(1840-1900)
These were monochromatic brick or stone buildings, highlighted by semicircular arches for window and door openings. The arch is used decoratively to enrich corbel tables along the eaves and courses, marking horizontal divisions. The arches and capitals of columns are carved with geometrical medieval moldings.

Otto Wagner
(1841-1918)
His architectural style predated Art Deco. He designed the Majolika Haus, Vienna (1898), an original Art Noveau building in which a floral design covers the façade. He also designed the Sezession Exhibition Building, Vienna, Austria, (1899); and the Postal Savings Bank, Vienna, (1904), with a high vaulted central hall with tapering metal supports.

Gothic Revival

Dankmar Adler
(1844-1900)
German-born engineer, who moved to Chicago in 1854, and became a partner of Louis H. Sullivan. The Auditorium Building, Chicago (1886), was their first joint commission. In 1889, the firm employed the young Frank Lloyd Wright.

Daniel Hudson Burnham
(1846-1912)
An American architect who partnered with John Wellborn Root. The firm was responsible for starting the Chicago School of Skyscraper Designs. He first designed the Monadnock Building, then the Reliance Building, both in Chicago. The latter is based on a metal steel skeleton and terra-cotta cladding. He also designed the Flatiron Building, in New York City.

William R. Mead
(1846-1928)
Partner in the New York firm of McKim, Mead & White.

Charles Follen McKim
(1847-1909)
His bold design is best expressed in Pennsylvania Station, New York City, (now demolished). Another of his important works is the layout and design of the Columbia University campus in New York City.

John Wellborn Root
(1850-1891)
American architect who formed a partnership with Daniel Burnham, which influenced the development of the Chicago School.

John Eisenman
(1851-1924)
Best known for his design of the Cleveland Arcade, Cleveland, (1882), with its two nine-story round arched blocks flanking a galleried iron-and-glass façade.

Stick Style (1855-1900)
An almost purely American residential style characterized by exposed framing overlaid on clapboard in horizontal, vertical or diagonal patterns to suggest support. A western adaptation emerged later in the work of Greene and Greene and Bernard Maybeck. Heralded by some as "modern," it is characterized by horizontality, structural timber frames, and often with Japanese influences.

Antonio Gaudi y Cornet
(1852-1926)
One of the most original architectural talents, inspired by Islamic and Gothic sources, whose work is mainly found in Barcelona, Spain. Casa Vicens (1878) was his first work, a suburban house decorated with polychrome tiles and sinuous ironwork. The commission for La Sagrada Familia church (1884) with completed transcept façades, with its extraordinary ceramic-covered spires, is his most fantastic work. The Palacio Guell (1885) is dominated by a pair of parabolic arches at the entrance and topped by chimneys encrusted with colored tiles. Casa Batlo (1905) has a unique tile roof and tile façade, and Casa Mila has an undulating façade and huge ceramic-covered chimney pots on the roof.

P.V. Jensen Klint
(1853-1930)
His Grundvig Church in Copenhagen (1913), is one of the most imaginative of Scandinavian designs, with a Gothic flavor. Built entirely of brick, it features a steep stepped-gabled façade resembling organ pipes.

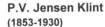

Stanford White
(1853-1906)
Partner in the firm of McKim, Mead & White. The buildings produced by the firm were the most appreciated of their time. He designed the Washington Square Arch in New York City, and houses for Louis Comfort Tiffany, Charles Dana Gibson, and Joseph Pulitzer.

William Holabird
(1854-1923)
Designed the Tacoma Building, Chicago, Illinois, a 12-story building that established the Chicago School of Architects as leaders in skyscraper design.

Hendrik Petrus Berlage
(1856-1934)
Designed the Amsterdam Stock Exchange of brick, using a stone trim, which was a fresh interpretation of the Romanesque style.

Cass Gilbert
(1859-1934)
Designed the Woolworth Building, New York City, which was the tallest building in American for 17 years. It was ornamented with Gothic details.

Louis H. Sullivan
(1856-1924)
Leader of the Chicago School of Architecture and a pioneer in skyscraper design. The Auditorium Building, Chicago (1887), was his first major work. It is notable for an early and very personal use of Art Nouveau interior decoration. The Carson Pirie Scott Department Store, Chicago (1900), the architect's last work, was designed with a horizontal emphasis, and demonstrated his interest in organically inspired façade ornament.

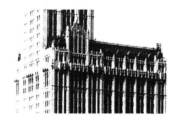

Victor Horta
(1861-1947)
The leading architect in the Art Nouveau style (c. 1900). The Tassel House, Brussels, Belgium, was his first major work in the Art Nouveau style. The L'Innovation department store, Brussels, Belgium (1901), had a large metal and glass Art Nouveau façade.

Rudolf Steiner
(1861-1925)
An Austria-Hungarian philosopher, artist, scientist, and architect. His Geotheanum, Dornach, Switzerland (1913), was the epitome of Expressionism, with a strong Symbolist and Jugendstil flavor. It was built of reinforced concrete.

Bernard Maybeck
(1862-1937)
Designed the Christian Science Church, Berkley, California, in a mixture of styles. He also designed the Palace of Fine Arts, San Francisco, for the Pan Pacific International Exposition of 1915. The Expo was demolished, but the Palace remains, now rebuilt out of permanent materials.

Victorian Gothic (1860-1890)
In this colorful style, materials of different colors and textures are juxtaposed, creating decorative bands highlighting corners, arches and arcades. Materials most often used are ornamental pressed bricks, terracotta tile and incised carvings of foliated and geometric patterns. Openings have straight heads as well as pointed Gothic arched heads. In timber frame buildings the gable, porch and eave trim is massive and strong. This is in sharp contrast to the lighter curvilinear gingerbread type trim of the Gothic Revival. This style was the epitome of Victorian.

French (1860-1875)

Generally called "mansard" for its characteristic roof structure, the style was based on those in vogue during the reign of Napoleon. Height was emphasized with elaborate chimneys, dormer windows and circular windows protruding from the roof. Projecting pavilions, undulating facades, and classical ornament produced a true three-dimensional effect. The style often became asymmetrical ·

Frank Lloyd Wright
(1867-1959)

Originator of the Organic style, as demonstrated in many innovative works. Unity Temple, Oak Park, Illinois (1906), was a concrete church with a complex interior space on several levels. The Millard house, Pasadena, California (1923), was built of decorative pre-cast concrete blocks. Fallingwater, Bear Run, Pennsylvania, was cantilevered out over a waterfall in horizontal sections. It was not unlike the European International Style in elevation, but was three- dimensional in actuality. The Johnson Wax Building, Racine, Wisconsin (1937), features the innovative use of materials, such as glass tubes for skylights. The Guggenheim Museum in New York City (1943-1960), is one of his best-known works, with the exterior expressing the interior arrangement.

Willis Jefferson Polk
(1867-1924)

An American architect working in San Francisco, influenced by McKim, Mead & White. He assisted Daniel Burnham in the city plan for San Francisco (1904). The Hallidie Building, San Francisco (1917), is his most distinctive work, having a fully glazed curtain-wall hung from the main framed structure, the first of its kind.

Louis Christian Mulgardt
(1866-1942)

American architect of German descent, influenced by the Arts and Crafts movement. In the 1920's, he produced a series of fantastic proposals for San Francisco, including habitable piers and bridges connected by 24-lane tiered motorways.

Joseph Olhbrich
(1867-1908)

Co-founder of the Vienna Sezession movement. He designed the Ernst Ludwig Haus, Darmstadt, in the Art Nouveau style, reminiscent of Macintosh, and the Wedding Chapel and Exhibition Hall, Darmstadt, Germany.

Hector Guimard
(1867-1942)

Designed the metro stations of Paris with an Art Nouveau motif.

Charles Sumner Greene
(1868-1957)
American-born architect who studied at MIT and set up practice with his brother Henry in Pasadena, California. They used projecting roofs, flat gables, and timber construction. The most well known is the Gambel House in Pasadena, (1908).

Henry Mather Greene
(1870-1954)
Partner with Charles Sumner Greene, his brother.

Charles Rennie Macintosh
(1868-1928)
His first major Art Nouveau work was the Cranston Tea Room, Edinburgh, Scotland. He also designed the Glaslow School of Art, a highly original Art Nouveau design.

Peter Behrens
(1869-1938)
Designed the AEG Turbine Factory, Berlin (1908). It was a strictly functional factory, constructed of concrete, steel, and glass, without ornamentation.

Bertam G. Goodue
(1869-1924)
American architect, in partnership with Ralph Cram from 1892 to 1913. On his own, he designed St. Bartholomew's Church, New York City, the last in a Byzantine Romanesque style. His most well-known work is the Nebraska State Capital, Lincoln, (1920).

Hans Poelzig
(1869-1936)
Berlin-born architect, later city architect of Dresden, Germany. He designed the Grosse Schauspielhaus, Berlin (1919), and Chemical Plant, Luban (1912). As a professor, he produced several fantastic Expressionist designs, all unrealized.

Albert Kahn
(1869-1942)
German-born American architect who formed a practice with his brothers Julius and Moritz, and designed industrial buildings for automobile manufacturers Packard, Ford, and Chrysler.

Sir Edwin Landseer Lutyens
(1869-1944)
Important English architect, who designed the plan for the city of New Delhi, India (1912). His later work includes many commercial bank buildings in London (1920).

Tony Garnier
(1869-1948)
While a student in Rome, published *Cite Industrial Designs* in 1918, which constituted a revolutionary plan for a model town of 35,000. This publication influenced Le Corbusier and other Modernists.

Irving Gill
(1870-1936)
Designed the Dodge House, Los Angeles, a composition of white-painted blocks reminiscent of contemporary European houses, similar to the cubistic style of Adolph Loos.

Adolf Loos
(1870-1933)
Primarily a designer of houses. He disclaimed all forms of ornament. He designed the Kartner Bar, Vienna, Austria, and the Gustav Sheu House, Vienna, a typically box-like exterior with rectangular windows of various sizes.

Josef Hoffman
(1870-1956)
Designed the Stocklet House, Brussels, Belgium (1905). The exterior was enhanced with marble and bronze, while the interior featured mosaics by Gustav Klimt.

Richardsonian (1870-1900)
A straightforward treatment of stone, broad roof planes and a select grouping of door and window openings was the most characteristic features of this style. It was named for Henry Hobson Richardson, and featured a heavy massive appearance with a simplicity of form and rough masonry. The overall effect depends on mass, volume, and scale rather than enriched or decorative detailing. However, there is a rich detailing on the capitals of columns. The facade is punctuated with deep window recesses. The entry is characterized by a very large arched opening without columns or piers for support.

George Elmslie
(1871-1952)
Partnered with William Greg Purcell (1880-1965), best known for their houses of the Prairie School style. Elmslie worked briefly with Louis Sullivan on the Carson Pirie Scott store in Chicago.

Marion Mahony Griffin
(1871-1961)
Worked for Frank Lloyd Wright in Oak Park, Illinois, and was responsible for many of the drawings of Wright's work published in the *Wasmuth Portfolio* of 1910.

Eastlake (1870-1880)

In this style, porch posts, railings and balusters were characterized by a massive and robust quality. These members were turned on a mechanical lathe. Large curved brackets, scrolls and other stylized elements are often placed at every corner, turn or projection along the facade. Added to this are perforated gables, carved panels and a profusion of spindles and latticework found along the porch eaves.

Emery Roth
(1871-1948)
Designed the Helmsley Palace Hotel, New York City (1980), and the Pan Am building, in New York City, with Walter Gropius and Pietro Belluschi (1963).

Julia Morgan
(1872-1957)
American architect and engineer; the first woman to study at the Ecole des Beaux Arts, Paris, and California's first licensed woman architect. Her work includes several buildings for Mills College, Oakland, California, including the reinforced concrete campanile (1903) and the Library and Gymnasium (1907). She designed the buildings at San Simeon, California (1919), for William Randolph Hearst (1851).

Robert Maillart
(1872-1940)
Graduated as a structural engineer and built his first of 40 reinforced-concrete bridges in 1901. He contributed to the design of mushroom slab construction in high structures, where the columns, beams and floors are integral.

Eliel Saarinen
(1873-1950)
Designed the Helsinki Railway Station, built of rugged granite and inspired by the designs of the Vienna Sezession.

John Russell Pope
(1874-1937)
A disciple of McKim, Mead & White. He trained at the Ecole des Beaux Arts, Paris. Designed the Jefferson Memorial (1937) and the National Gallery of Art (1937), both in Washington, D.C., and the Sculpture Hall, Tate Gallery, London (1937). The latter contains the sculpture from the Parthenon in Athens - the Elgin Marbles.

Auguste Perret
(1874-1955)
His 25 Rue Franklin apartment house in Paris (1903), was an early example of re-inforced concrete frame construction. He designed the Garage Ponthiew in Paris (1906), and Note-Dame le Raincy (1922), a hall-church design built with reinforced-concrete vaults and walls glazed with stained glass.

Walter Burley Griffin
(1876-1937)
He worked in Chicago with Frank Lloyd Wright before being appointed director for the design and construction of the Federal Capital at Canberra, Australia in 1913. Here he also designed many major works with his wife, Marion Lucy Mahoney (1871-1961).

Arts and Crafts (1880-1891)

The aim of this movement was to restore a feeling of creativity to the decorative arts, and indirectly to architecture. It exercised profound influence on the development of new ideas and methods of work over all of Europe. Architects such as Henry Van de Velde and Charles Rennie Mackintosh had a very strong influence on this movement. It abandoned the stylistic imitation of the nineteenth century, and its preference for continuous forms laid the groundwork for the creative works of the Art Nouveau and Jugendstil styles that followed.

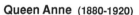

Queen Anne (1880-1920)

The elements and forms of many styles are manipulated into an exuberant visual display in this most varied and decoratively rich style. The asymmetrical compositions consists of a variety of forms, textures and materials. The main elements include towers and turrets, tall chimneys, projecting pavilions, porches, bays and verandas. Colored glass panels are found in the windows.

Art Nouveau (1880-1910)

This movement in European architecture and applied arts, was developed principally in France and Belgium. It was characterized by flowing and sinuous organic and dynamic forms, naturalistic ornament and a strict avoidance of historical traits. Other names for the style include; Le Modern Style (France), Jugendstil (Austria), Stile Liberty (Italy), Modernismo (Spain), and Sezession (Germany). The best architects of this epoch were individualists, including Hector Guimard, Victor Horta, Antonio Gaudi, August Perret, H.P. Berlage, Otto Wagner and Peter Behrens.

The style drew on the Baroque, Gothic and Moorish traditions, but was mainly unbounded by rules, and was only concerned with the creation of a good building. Art Nouveau exploited the machine and revelled in the decorative possibilities of tiles and wrought iron. It never advanced far beyond domestic design, and was particularly influencial in interiors, furniture and other art objects.

It was an individualistic and anti-historical movement and expressed an essentially decorative trend that highlighted the curved line. This linear quality was expressed in asymmetrical forms, which was a deliberate attempt to put an end to imitations of past styles. In its place was a free type of architecture which integrated arts and crafts with architectural forms.

Bruno Taut
(1880-1938)
German architect who became an advisor to the German Garden City Movement. His glass pavilion, Werkbund Exposition, Cologne (1914) is his most celebrated work, a paradigm of Expressionism. He published many books.

Antonio Sant' Elia
(1880-1916)
He studied architecture in Milan, was influenced by Otto Wagner's Vienna School. He exhibited work with fellow student Mario Chiattone, and published a manifesto on Futurism in the exhibition catalog.

Raymond Mathewson Hood
(1881-1934)
Won the competition with John Mead Howells in 1922 to design the Chicago Tribune Tower, Chicago, a highpoint in Beaux-Arts eclecticism with a Gothic superstructure. He designed the Daily News building in the Art Deco Style (1929), and the McGraw-Hill building (1930), both in New York City.

William Van Alen
(1882-1954)
Designed the Chrysler Building, New York City (1928), in a Moderne style, which combined massive forms, inspired by ancient architecture, with Art Deco motifs and streamlined shapes. He used steel and aluminum to celebrate the machine age. The Art Deco upper part incorporates eagle-head and radiator-cap gargoyles, as well as a series of semicircular forms recalling hubcaps.

Walter Gropius
(1883-1969)
His design for the Bauhaus, Dessau, Germany (1925), was the first example of the new International-style architecture to be built. He left Germany in 1828. He designed the Graduate Center, Harvard University, Cambridge (1949), while professor of Architecture at Harvard.

Theo van Doesburg
(1883-1931)
He began his career as a painter, and established the de Stijl movement with J. J. P. Oud. He later taught at the Bauhaus.

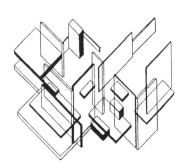

Michael de Klerk
(1884-1923)
Designed Elgen Haard Housing, Amsterdam, one of several housing estates, with his colleague Piet Kramer (1881-1961). It was built of brick and featured skillfully curved corners and details.

Ludwig Mies Van der Rohe
(1886-1969)
Designed the German Pavilion, Barcelona Exhibition (1929), built on one level with carefully articulated space, all in high-quality materials. The Tugendhat House, Brno Switzerland (1930), had the living space divided only by screen walls. Mies moved to the United States. in 1938, and every tall glazed office building in the world bears his influence. The Seagram Building, New York (1956), with Philip Johnson, was considered the culmination of Mies's streamlined style; it was a rectangular slab of bronze, marble, and gray-tinted glass.

Eric Mendelsohn
(1887-1953)
Designed the Einstein Tower, Potsdam, a highly plastic building. Its design is an outcome of expressionist demands. He also designed the Luckenwalde Hat factory (1920), and the Schoken Department stores at Stuttgart, Germany (1926), using new forms for a new function.

William Marinus Dudok
(1884-1974)
Designed the Snellius School in Hilversum, Holland, as compositions of asymmetrical rectangular blocks, predating the International Style.

Eric Gunnar Asplund
(1885-1940)
One of the most eminent of Swedish architects. He adopted Neo classicism, and designed the City Library, Stockholm (1920), which had Architectonic shapes reduced to basic rectangles and cylinders.

Vladimir Tatlin
(1885-1953)
Designed the Memorial to the Third International. It was a Constructivist architectural fantasy, a spiral leaning tower. Constructivism was a short-lived ideal in Russia.

Le Corbusier
(1887-1965)
Pseudonym of Charles-Edouard Jenneret, the most influential of twentieth century architects. The Villa Savoy, Poissy (1929), is typical of his residential designs, freely planned with geometric shapes and using modern construction techniques. He called such houses "machines for living." The Pavilion Suisse, Paris (1932), was built on stilts, and featured the curved walls, cubist blocks, and a random rubble wall to contrast with the white concrete. The Unite d'Habitation, Marseilles (1946), shows emphasis on mass and on the untreated concrete. The proportions for his buildings were worked out on his 'modular system'. He designed Notre-Dame-du-Haut, Ronchamps, France (1959), which is molded in concrete, to create a huge sculptural form penetrated by windows placed at random. Chandigarh, East Punjab, was planned as a new state capital,

Gerrit Drietvelt
(1888-1964)
Architect and member of the de Stijl group of artists which included painter Piet Mondrian. Their buildings were intricate, delicately balanced compositions of line and plane. The Schroder House, Utrecht (1924), was small but unusual, reminiscent in its intersecting planes and angles of a Mondrian painting.

Iakov Georgievich Chernikov
(1889-1951)
Russian-born architect, teacher, writer. His work focused on architectural compositions in perspective, illustrating forms and structures of the imagination, following the Constructivist principles.

Rudolph Michael Schindler
(1887-1953)
Born in Vienna, he was influenced early by Otto Wagner. He later worked for Wright in Chicago, but his work remains reminiscent of the de Stijl movement, in his Lovell Beach house, Newport Beach, California (1926).

Ralph Thomas Walker
(1889-1973)
An American architect best know for his Art Deco skyscrapers, including the Barclay-Vesey Telephone Building (1923) and the Irving Trust Building (1929), both in New York City.

Konstandin Melnikov
(1890-1974)
Russian architect whose work anticipated certain aspects of Deconstructivism, which gained him popularity among the avant-garde. He is mostly associated with the Constructivists.

Hugh Ferriss
(1889-1962)
Distinguished American architectural delineator and visionary. His images of futuristic buildings were published in the *Metropolis of Tomorrow* (1929), which impacted architecture in the 1930s.

Frederick John Kiesler
(1890-1965)
Vienna-born American visionary architect. His "endless house" encapsulated his organic ideas of curves and continuous wall and ceiling planes as a contrast to the rectangular grid.

Charles Franklin Murphy
(1890-1985)
Worked with Daniel Burnham and the Chicago school. He produced several Chicago office buildings, and with partner Helmut Jahn designed O-Hare International Airport (1965) and the Exhibition building at McCormick Place (1971).

Sullivanesque (1890-1920)
This style was named for Louis Henry Sullivan, noted as much for his stylized geometrical ornament as for his simple multistory forms that ended in bold cornices. His skyscrapers were designed as if they were classical columns. To emphasize height he used vertical rows of windows separated by ornamented bands. The columns were uninterrupted to express the height, much the same as fluting. The massive decorative cornice resembled the capital. There was an intricate weaving of linear and geometric forms with stylized foliage ornamentation. Facades are pierced with bold geometric forms and large arched openings. The wall surface is highlighted with extensive low-relief sculptural ornamentation in terra cotta.

Lloyd Wright
(1890-1978)
Elder son of Frank Lloyd Wright. Trained in his father's studio, he helped prepare drawings for the *Wasmuth Portfolio* (1918). He worked on several concrete block houses and the Barnsdall Residence in Los Angeles. His later work included the Swedenborg Memorial Wayfarer's Chapel, Palos Verdes.

Gio Ponti
(1891-1979)
Italian architect and designer, influenced by the Sezession Movement and Otto Wagner. He was the founder-director of *Domus* magazine (1928). He worked with Nervi in the design of the Pirelli Tower in Milan, Italy (1956), and designed the Museum of Modern Art in Denver (1972).

Commercial (1890-1915)
This was the skeletal, rectangular style of the first five to fifteen story skyscrapers, brought to full form in Chicago, New York, and Philadelphia. It was characterized by flat roofs and little ornament, except slight variations in the spacing of windows. The extensive use of glass was made possible by the steel-frame construction that could bear the structural loads that masonry could not.

Western Stick (1890-1920)
This adaptation was characterized by a gently pitched gable roof that extends well beyond the wall and by projecting balconies. A unique feature is the exposed stick-like rafters that project along the roof. Window lintels, railings and other beams extend beyond vertical posts. Pegs are used to join the members, and the ends are rounded off, as are the corners of posts and beams.

Richard Josef Neutra
(1892-1970)
Vienna-born architect working with Adolph Loos and Eric Mendelsohn. He met Louis Sullivan and Frank Lloyd Wright, and in 1925 formed an association in Los Angeles with Rudolph Schindler. He designed many homes for notable Hollywood names.

Mission (1890-1920)
The characteristic style is simplicity of form. Round arches were supported by piers. The roof eaves extend beyond the wall. Towers, curvilinear gables and small balconies were used for large buildings. The only ornamentation is a plain string course that outlines arches or gables or balconies.

Beaux Arts Classicism
(1890-1920)
Large and grandiose compositions with an exuberance of detail and a variety of stone finishes, all characterize this style. Classical columns were often grouped in pairs with enriched molding and free-standing statuary. It had pronounced cornices topped with a parapet. It ushered in an era of academic revivals, and was principally used for public buildings. One of the most notable features is the use of monumental flights of steps.

Jacobus J. P. Oud
(1890-1963)
His Hook of Holland Housing Estate in Rotterdam expresses the rigid discipline of the de Stijl artists.

Mario B. Chiattone
(1891-1957)
Studied in Milan, became a member of the Futurist Movement, and with fellow student Sant'Elia exhibited a collection of drawings in Milan called *Structures for a Modern Metropolis* (1914).

Pier Luigi Nervi
(1891-1979)
Italian civil engineer, best known for his reinforced-concrete structures. He created a structure for the Exhibition Hall, Turin, Italy (1947), and the Palazzo Dello Sports (1958) in Rome, where an immense dome floats over the space.

De Stijl (1892-1921)
This movement began in Holland with two branches of the avant-garde, the Purists and Expressionists. It took its name from the magazine which published its manifestos. It was influenced by Cubist painting. Right angles and smooth walls were the order of the day. The cube served as the point of departure, as an elementary expression of space, into which the internal walls continued. The designed space, which was the room, opened out on all sides into the "universal space."

Norman Bel Geddes
(1893-1958)
American designer identified with the Streamled style. Designed the General Motors Pavilion at the New York World's Fair (1939). He produced many interiors and developed a scheme for prefabricated housing.

Han Scharoun
(1893-1972)
German architect influenced by Expressionism. His most celebrated work is the Hall for the Berlin Philharmonic Orchestra, which shows his commitment to Organic architecture.

Pierre Jeanneret Gris
(1896-1967)
Swiss architect, a relative of Le Corbusier, who joined the office of Perret and worked with Le Corbusier on designs and town planning schemes. He was a protagonist of the International Modern Movement, but was obscured by the fame of Le Corbusier.

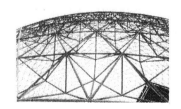

Wallace Kirkman Harrison
(1895-1981)

Formed one of the most successful practices in America with Raymond Hood. He worked on Rockefeller, Center, New York City, and designed the United Nations Headquarters with Le Corbusier; Phoenix Mutual Life Insurance building, Hartford; Lincoln Center, New York City, and the gigantic South Mall Government Complex in Albany.

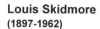

William Wilson Wurster
(1895-1973)

As principal of Wurster, Bernardi and Emmons he produced many works in what was called the Bay Region Style. He designed many university buildings in California, and Ghiradelli Square in San Francisco (1962).

Richard Buckminster Fuller
(1895-1983)

Developed the geodesic dome, protecting an interior space, suitable for any arrangement, by a vast "space frame."

John Ogden Merrill
(1896-1975)

Partner in the firm of Skidmore, Owings and Merrill (SOM).

Louis Skidmore
(1897-1962)

Founded Skidmore, Owings and Merrill in Chicago in 1936 which was organized on teamwork and incorporated ideas from business practice. SOM won fame for Lever House in New York City. Later work included the John Hancock Center, Chicago, many projects in Saudi Arabia (1982) and Canary Wharf developments in London (1990).

William Lescaze
(1896-1969)

His Savings Fund Building, Philadelphia, was one of the first skyscrapers designed in the International Style.

Alvar Alto
(1898-1978)

Built Viipuri Public Library with an undulating timber roof (1929). His Paimio Sanitorium is one of the first hospitals to be built in the International Style.

Peter Belluschi
(1899-1994)

Italian-born architect and engineer, who showed an inclination to International Style Modernism. His Equitable Life Assurance Building, Portland, Oregon (1944), was one of the first examples of an aluminum and glass curtain-wall enclosing a concrete frame tower. He became dean of the School of Architecture at MIT, Cambridge, Massachusetts.

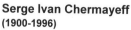

Eduardo Torroja
(1899-1961)

Spanish architect and engineer of concrete shells. Studied civil engineering. Most of his designs employed folded, undulating, or warped shapes.

Serge Ivan Chermayeff
(1900-1996)

Born in Russia, emigrated to England in 1910 and worked as a designer before joining Eric Mendelsohn. He designed many Modern Movement buildings. He emigrated to America in 1940.

Organic (1900-1920)

There are several theories that apply to organic architecture. The first derives from ancient Greek and Roman architecture, and was further developed during the Renaissance. The Greeks based the proportions that control design on the proportions of the human figure. This was further developed by Vitruvius. Vasari held that architecture must appear organic like the body, and Michelangelo held that a knowledge of the human figure led to a comprehension of architecture.

The second theory is the application of organic life to design. In natural organisms there is a harmony of parts in relation to the whole which appears to be conditioned by the work the organism is designed to perform. Some of the proponents of this philosophy includes Henry Van de Velde, Hector Guimard, Victor Horta, Antonio Gaudi, and Louis Sullivan.

Functionalism (1900-1950)

This design philosophy asserts that the form of a building should follow its function, reveal its structure, and express the nature of the material. It should be devoid of decoration, symbolism or apparent aesthetic consideration. It should express the building's practical purposes.

Actually, there is no other architectural principle that can claim a more ancient and distinguished tradition. Form has followed function since the Paleolithic cave dwellers; it followed function in Roman forts, in medieval castles, and in modern office buildings. In short, functionalism is as old as building itself.

Neo Classicism (1900-1920)

This revival style was based primarily on the Greek and to a lesser extent on the Roman orders. These were symmetrically arranged buildings of monumental proportions. The arch was not used and enriched moldings are rare. The preference was for simple geometric forms and smooth surfaces. The design was based on the assembly of a number of disparate volumes.

Louis I. Kahn
(1901-1974)

Born in Estonia, settled in the United States and became known for the Yale Art Gallery, New Haven (1951). The Salk Institute Laboratories (1959) was an important work, as was the Kimbell Art Museum, Fort Worth (1967), and the Phillips Exeter Academy Library, Exeter, New Hampshire (1967). Richards Laboratories in Philadelphia has a bold silhouetting of towers. His last work was the National Assembly of Bangladesh, Dacca (1962).

Josep Luis Sert
(1902-1983)

Catalonian architect who worked with Le Corbusier. He settled in the United States in 1939 and became Dean of Faculty at the Graduate School of Design, and Chairman of Architecture at Harvard University (1953). He designed the U.S. Embassy, Baghded, Iraq, and the Miro Foundation Building, Barcelona, Spain (1972).

Eward Durrell Stone
(1902-1978)

Absorbed the Modern Movement working on Rockefeller Center, and designed the interior of Radio City Music Hall. His U.S. Embassy, New Delhi, India (1954), and the Kennedy Center for the Performing Arts, Washington, DC (1961), were axial and symmetrical, and paraphrased the Classical movement.

Marcel Breuer
(1902-1981)

An important Modernist, born in Hungary. He taught at the Bauhaus at Weimar, Germany, and invented a series of furniture designs using bent steel tubes finished in chrome. His latest work was the Whitney Museum of Art in New York City.

Victor David Gruen
(1903-1980)

Viennese architect, who settled in the United States in 1938, starting his own firm in Los Angeles, specializing in shopping centers, such as Northland Center in Detroit.

Expressionism (1903-1925)

This Northern European style did not treat buildings as purely functional structures, but also as sculptural objects in their own right. Works that were typical of this style were done by Gaudi in Spain, Klint in Denmark, Mendelsohn and Poelzig in Germany.

Nathaniel A. Owings
(1903-1984)

Partner in the firm of Skidmore, Owings and Merrill (SOM). Some noteworthy projects of the firm are Lever House, New York City, (1952), Inland Steel Building, Chicago (1958), One Chase Plaza New York City (1962), the Beinecke Rare Book Library, Yale University, New Haven (1963), The Air Force Academy chapel, Colorado Springs (1963), Circle Campus, University of Illinois, Chicago (1965), John Hancock Center, Chicago (1970), Weyerhauser Headquarters, Tacoma (1971), and Sears Tower, Chicago (1974).

Alden B. Dow
(1904-1983)

An American architect, worked with Frank Lloyd Wright in 1933, before setting up his own practice in 1935. His later work represents his own individual style.

Kunio Mayekawa
(1905-1986)

Member of the Japanese group Werkbund. He worked for Le Corbusier. His Harimi Apartments, Tokyo (1957), carry over Japanese domestic traditions into the dimensions of a modern skyscraper.

Bruce Alonzo Goff
(1904-1982)

One of the most idiosyncratic architects in America, who used found materials such as coal, rope, and glass cullets. His best-known works are the Ford House in Aurora, Illinois (1948), the Bavinger house in Norman, Oklahoma (1950), and the Price House in Bartlesville, Oklahoma (1956), all of which were treated with great individuality.

Philip Johnson
(1906-)

His New Canaan house saw the style of Mies Van der Rohe reach its ultimate development. It is a glazed box in which only the bathroom in enclosed. Other works include the Museum of Modern Art additions and sculpture garden, the New York State Theater at Lincoln Center, New York City, and Kline Science Center (with Richard Foster) at Yale University, New Haven (1965). His works with John Burgee include: the IDS Center, Minneapolis, (1972), the Boston Public Library addition, Boston (1972), Pennzoil Place, Houston (1976), the Crystal Cathedral, Garden Grove, California (1980), Transco Tower, (with Morris Aubrey), Houston (1983), and the AT&T Building, (with John Burgee), New York City (1984).

Carlo Scarpa
(1906-1978)
Italian architect, practicing in Venice; a subscriber to the Modern Movement. Later, his work focused on exhibitions, galleries, and museums.

George Hellmuth
(1907-)
Design partner in the firm of Hellmuth Obata and Kassabaum, most noted for the Lambert-St. Louis Municipal Airport Terminal Building, St. Louis, Missouri (1955) (with Minuro Yamasaki).

Charles Eames
(1907-1978)
His own house in Santa Monica was influential because of its construction from prefabricated standard components in a totally modern style.

Oscar Niemeyer
(1907-1989)
The Ministry of Health and Education, Rio de Janeiro, is a Modern-style tower block modified by sunbreaks, devised by Le Corbusier, the consultant architect. Niemeyer was interested in buildings as sculpture. Brasilia, Brazil (1960), was planned in the shape of a bird, with the parliamentary building at its head. The influence of Le Corbusier is evident.

Luigi Walter Moretti
(1907-1973)
Italian architect whose early work was in the Neoclassical style of Rationialist architecture. His most notable later work is the Watergate complex in Washington, DC (1960).

Lawrence Perkins
(1907-1982)
Founder of the Chicago-based firm of Perkins and Will.

Max Abramovitz
(1908-1963)
American architect educated at the Ecole des Beaux-Arts in Paris. He was a partner to Wallace K. Harrison.

Eero Saarinen
(1910-1961)
Finnish-born American architect, son of Eliel Saarinen. Projects include the General Motors Technical Institute, Warren, Michigan (1951), Kresge Auditorium at M.I.T. in Cambridge (1952), the David S. Ingalls Ice Hockey Rink at Yale University, New Haven, (1953), TWA Terminal at Kennedy International Airport, New York City (1956), Ezra Stiles and Morse College, Yale University, New Haven, (1958).

Gordon Bunshaft
(1909-1990)
Partner of the firm, Skidmore, Owings & Merrill. Designed Lever House, New York City (1952), a 21-story curtain-walled skyscraper slab set on a lower podium.

William Pereira
(1910-1990)
Founder of the Los Angeles-based firm of Pereira and Luckman, with Charles Luckman.

Matthew Nowicki
(1910-1951)
Polish architect who designed the Dorton Arena, North Carolina State Fair, Raleigh (1948), with two intersecting hyperbolic parabolas. He is regarded as a pioneer of such structural design. He worked with Saarinen on the master plan for Chandigarh, India.

Felix Candela
(1910-1981)
Designed the Church of the Miraculous Virgin, Narvarte, Mexico, an expressionist building made of concrete in the form of a hyperbolic paraboloid.

Viljo Revell
(1910-1964)
Finnish architect who studied with Alvar Alto, and made his name with the "Glass Palace" office building in Helsinki, Finland. He won the competition in 1958 for the Toronto City Hall, whose two curvilinear office towers contrast with the neighboring office structures.

Ernest Kump
(1911-1991)
His most notable project was Foothill College, Los Altos Hills, California (1961), consisting of 40 buildings on a 122-acre campus, all designed and built as a unit.

Minoru Yamasaki
(1912-1986)
American architect of Japanese descent. He and his partner George Hellmuth made their mark with the TWA Terminal at Lambert Airport, St. Louis. The Pruitt-Igoe public housing project, also in St. Louis, won several awards, but was detested by its inhabitants and later demolished. He used aluminum grille screens and other intricate detailing in high-rise structures. His twin towers for the World Trade Center in New York City are his landmark structures.

Hugh Asher Stubbins
(1912-)
In 1939, became assistant to Walter Gropius at Harvard, established his own practice in Cambridge (1940), and succeeded Gropius as chairman of the Department of Architecture. He designed the Congress Hall in Berlin (1957), and Citicorp Center in New York City (1978).

Bertrand Goldberg
(1913-)
Chicago architect most noted for the Hilliard Center Apartments (1966) and Marina City Apartments (1967), both in Chicago.

Kenzo Tange
(1913-)
Came from Kunio Mayekawa's office and was influenced by Le Corbusier, but drew on Japanese themes. The Hiroshima Peace Center and Museum was his first major project. Later work includes the National Gymnasium, Tokyo (1961), which was covered by a gigantic tensile catenary roof structure.

Joseph Esherick
(1914-)
San Francisco architect most noted for the renovation and redevelopment of the Cannery (1968), a retail complex on Fisherman's Wharf, San Francisco, and the Monterey Bay Aquarium, Monterey, California (1984).

Ralph Rapson
(1914-)
Minneapolis-based architect who began his career working with Eero Saarinen. Notable works include: Cedar Square West, Minneapolis (1974), and the Tyrone Guthrie Theater, Minneapolis (1963).

Lawrence Halprin
(1916-)
San Francisco-based landscape architect noted for his park designs employing cascading vegetation and waterfalls, as in the Seattle Freeway Park (1976).

Futurism (1914-1916)
A movement began with a publication of work by two young architects, Antonio Sant'Elia and Mario Chiattone who presented a series of designs for a city of the future. The manifesto proclaimed that architecture is breaking loose from tradition, starting from scratch. It had a preference for what is light, practical and ephemeral. These works were ultimately published, but no buildings were ever built.

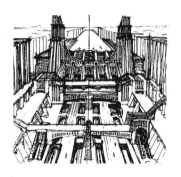

Vincent Kling
(1916-)
Philadelphia-based architect who designed the Municipal Services Building, Philadelphia (1965).

John Maclane Johansen
(1916-)
American architect, who worked with Marcel Breuer and SOM. He is best known for the circular Chancellery for the U.S. Embassy, Dublin (1958), and the Mummer's Theater, Oklahoma City, (1970).

Ieoh Ming Pei
(1917-)
Chinese-born American architect; studied with Walter Gropius at Harvard. He worked with William Zeckendorf's contracting firm. His notable later works include the National Center for Atmospheric Research, Boulder (1967), Christian Science Service Center, Boston (1971), John Hancock Tower, Boston (1975), extension to the National Gallery of Art, Washington, DC (1978), the Kennedy Library, Boston (1979), extension to the Louvre Museum, Paris (1983), Jacob Javits Convention Center, New York City (1986), and the Rock 'n' Roll Hall of Fame, Cleveland (1993).

Benjamin Thompson
(1918-)
Noted architect/developer; designed the Design Research Building, Cambridge, (1969), the large retail complex Harbor Place, Baltimore, (1980), and Faneuil Hall Marketplace and Quincy Market Restoration, Boston (1977), for the Rouse Company.

Jorn Utzon
(1918-)
Won the competition for the Sydney Opera House in Sydney, Australia in (1957), a controversial building with a sail-like roofline. It is architecture as sculpture, but strongly influenced by function.

Bruno Zevi
(1918-1999)
Italian architectural theorist who studied at Harvard University before returning to Italy. He published many books, including *Towards an Organic Architecture* (1945) and the *Modern Language of Architecture* (1973). He was opposed to International Modernism, Post-modernism, Classicism and Neoclassicism, advocating an organic approach.

Ettore Sottsass
(1917-)
Italian architect working in Milan; designed artifacts, exhibitions, and interiors. He has been classified as a Postmodernist Kitsch, merging consumer and popular culture with high design; Memphis furniture is an example.

Paul Marvin Rudolph
(1918-1997)
Studied with Walter Gropius at Harvard. He was chairman of Architecture at Yale University and designed the monumental Art and Architecture Building at New Haven (1958-1965), which was typical of his Brutalist architecture. Other works include the Government Center, Boston, (1962), and other college structures. Most of his later work was built in Indonesia.

Paolo Soleri
(1919-)
Italian-born American architect who worked for Frank Lloyd Wright (1947) before returning to Italy to build the Ceramics Factory, in Salerno (1953). He later established the Cosanti Foundation in Scottsdale (1955), and evolved the concept of Arcology, in which architecture and ecology are merged. Arcosanti, near Scottsdale, was commenced in 1970, representing the development of a city along his visionary ideas.

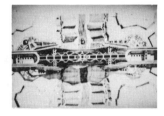

Bauhaus (1919-1937)

Walter Gropius established this famous school of design in Weimar, Germany. The term became virtually synonymous with modern teaching methods in architecture and the applied arts and with functional aesthetics for the industrial age. It epitomized the marriage of modern design, mass production and industrial design. This philosophy ruled modern architecture in an austere manner for nearly half a century.

Harry Weese
(1919-)
Principal of the Chicago-based firm; which designed office buildings for Chicago, and the metro subway stations for Washington, DC.

John Carl Warnecke
(1919-)
Successor to his father's firm of the same name. Designed the Hennepin County Government Center, Minneapolis (1976), consisting of twin 24-story towers with an enclosed atrium.

Constructivism (1920-1930)

Constructivism as a concept relates to any compact combination of different objects capable of being brought together into a single unified entity. This movement originated in Moscow. It was based on order, logic, structure, abstraction and geometry, primarily in sculpture, but with broad applications to architecture. The expression of construction was the base for all building design with emphasis on functional machine parts. Vladimar Tatlin's monument is the most notable example of this style.

The many industrial fantasies of Jacob Tchernikhov, published in 1933, shows buildings perched on cantilevered structures, suggesting construction for construction's sake. The tenet that has survived is the identity of efficient structure with beauty.

Romaldo Guirgola
(1920-)
Rome-born American architect, influenced primarily by the work of Louis Kahn. He designed the Volvo Headquarters, Stockholm, Sweden (1984), and the Parliament House of Australia, Canberra (1988). Partnered with American-born Ehrman Burkman Mitchell (1924-).

Modernistic (1920-1940)

A mode of ornamentation combining rectilinear patterns, zigzags, with geometrical curves characterize this style. One of the distinctive forms consisted of polychrome low-relief frames. Ornamentation around doors and windows and on panels stresses the verticality in skyscraper designs. Stepped setbacks are also common, reflecting local urban zoning ordinances.

Craig Ellwood
(1921-1992)
Designed mainly private residences and apartments of elegant proportions and detailing with standardized components of Mies Van der Rohe such as the Carson Roberts Building, Los Angeles (1961). Later he used exposed trusses at the Art Center College of Design, Pasadena (1970).

International Style(1920-1945)

The name given to the style of architecture which began to evolve in Europe and America shortly after the First World War still prevails today. It is characterized by an emphasis on function, and a rejection of traditional decorative motifs. It was a style devoid of regional characteristics. It was pioneered by Le Corbusier and spread to the Bauhaus, where it was the most influential.

It was characterized by flat roofs, smooth and uniform surfaces, large expanses of windows and projecting or cantilevered upper floors. The complete absence of ornamentation is typical. Cubistic shapes were fashionable. White is the preferred color. Horizontally emphasized windows turning round corners were favored. A puritanical asceticism was evident.

Roofs without eaves terminate flush with the plane of the wall. Wood and metal casement windows were set flush to the wall as well. Sliding windows were popular, and clerestory windows were also used. There were fixed panes of glass from floor to ceiling, and curtain-like walls of glass were common.

Popular building materials were reinforced concrete, steel frames, and an unprecedented use of pre-fabricated parts, since the style had its roots in industrial architecture. The resultant forms were much akin to cubist and abstract art.

Ulrich Franzen
(1921-)
Designed the Alley Theater, Houston (1968) and the Multi-categorical Animal Lab at Cornell University, Ithaca, New York (1974).

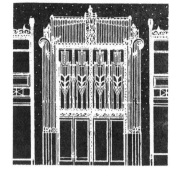

Eamonn Kevin Roche
(1922-)
Irish-born American architect, formed the successor firm to Eero Saarinen in the 1950's with John Gerald Dinkeloo (1918-1981). Their first work was the Oakland Museum (1961) a vast structure covering 4 city blocks. The best known is the Ford Foundation Headquarters, New York (1963) with a 12-story indoor atrium. The later work includes the extension to the Metropolitan Museum of Art, New York including the Pavilion for the Ancient Egyptian Temple of Dendur.

Victor Lundy
(1923-)
He trained under Walter Gropius and worked with Marcel Breuer. His best known work was the I. Miller Shoe Salon, Fifth Ave, New York City (1961) employing timber ribs and mirrors.

Gyo Obata
(1923-)
Partner in the firm of Hellmuth Obata and Kassabaum, noted for the Chapel Priory of St. Mary, St. Louis (1962), the National Air and Space Museum, Washington, DC (1976), the renovation of Union Station, St. Louis (1985), and the Dallas/Ft. Worth Airport (1973).

Arthur Charles Erickson
(1924-)
Canadian architect who gained international recognition with his plan for the central covered mall, Vancouver, Canada (1963). He was influenced by Le Corbusier, Kahn, and Rudolph.

John Calvin Portman, Jr.
(1924-)
American architect/developer known for his large urban buildings, including Peachtree Center (1961) and the Hyatt Regency Hotel (1967), both in Atlanta. He also designed Rockefeller West in San Francisco (1975).

Bruce Graham
(1925-)
Design partner in the Chicago office of SOM. He designed the John Hancock Building and the Sears Tower.

Gunnar Birkirts
(1925-)
Latvian-born American architect, much influenced by Eero Saarinen. He designed the Federal Reserve Bank, Minneapolis (1973), the IBM Corporate Computer Center, Sterling Forest, New York (1972), and the Museum of Glass, Corning, New York (1976).

Charles Willard Moore
(1925-1995)
A leading figure of Post modernism. Architectural history played a part in his designs which are tempered with fancy, myth, and evocative motifs. These are typified in the Piazza d'Italia, New Orleans, Louisiana (1975).

Art Deco **(1925-1940)**
Stimulated by an exhibition in Paris, this style drew its inspiration from Art Nouveau, American Indian art, Cubism, the Bauhaus, and Russian ballet. Among some of the well known architects was J.P. Oud and Eric Mendelsohn. It was the style of Odeon cinemas, of ocean liners, and hotel interiors. It has been called "modernistic," and it reconciled mass production with sophisticated design. It influenced skyscraper designs like the Chrysler building in New York City.

The stylistic elements were eclectic, and included mostly austere forms. It exhibited a free interpretation and a strong attempt at individuality. It was characterized by a linear, hard edge or angular composition with stylized decoration. The facades of buildings are often arranged in a series of setbacks, emphasizing the geometric form. Strips of windows with decorative spandrels add to the composition. Hard-edge low relief ornamentation around door and window openings and along the roof edges or parapets are common. Ornamental detailing is often in the same material as the building, or in contrasting metals, or in glazed bricks or mosaic tiles.

Style 42

Frei Otto
(1925-)

German architect and pioneer of the suspended tent roof. He used the idea for the West German Pavilion, Expo '67, Montreal, Canada (1967), and for the Olympic Park, Munich, Germany (1967). He published the book *Tensile Structures* in 1991.

James Frazer Stirling
(1926-1992)

Scots architect, influenced by Le Corbusier. Fell into the category of Brutalism in the Engineering Block building, University of Leicester, England (1959). His later work became increasingly eclectic and expressive and contained illusions to historical themes.

Cesar Pelli
(1926-)

Argentine-born American architect who worked for Eero Saarinen before becoming director of design for Daniel, Mann, Johnson & Mendenhall in1964, and later the design partner, Gruen Associates. He set up his own practice in New Haven (1977). The Pacific Design Center, Los Angeles (1971), brought his name to notice. He designed the Winter Garden and World Financial Center at the World Trade Center, New York City (1981), the Canary Wharf Tower, London (1986), and the huge Petronas Twin Towers, Kuala Lampur, Malaysia (1991).

Robert Charles Venturi
(1925-)

An American Post modernist who set up practice with John Rausch (1930-) and later with wife Denise Scott Brown (1930-), and later still with Steven Izenour (1930-). Early work included the Seattle Art Museum (1991) and the Museum of Contemporary Art, San Diego (1996).

CIAM (Congres Internationaux d'Architecture Moderne)
(1928)

A declaration signed by 24 architects, representing France (6), Switzerland (6), Germany (3), Holland (3), Italy (2), Spain (2), Austria (1), and Belgium (1), emphasized *building* rather than architecture. Advocated the introduction of efficient production methods in the building industry.

Eberhard H. Zeidler
(1926-)

German-born architect, trained at the Bauhaus and later settled in Canada. Best known for the enormous Eaton Center, Toronto (1969), Ontario Place, Toronto (1968), and Queens Quay Terminal Warehouse, Toronto (1981), and the Vancouver Convention Center (1997).

Frank O. Gehry
(1929-)

Canadian-born American architect, settled in Santa Monica, where he built several houses. He specialized in using materials in an unusual way. Major early works include the California Aerospace Museum, Santa Monica (1982), and the Watt Disney Concert Hall, Los Angeles (1989). The recent work includes the Weisman Center Art Museum, Minneapolis, and the Guggenheim Museum, Bilbao, Spain (1991).

Kiyonori Kikutake
(1928-)

Japanese architect and a leading light in Metabolism. His Sky House, Tokyo (1958), made his reputation. His proposed Marina City Project (1958), extending cities into the sea, was later partially realized at Aquapolis, Okinawa (1975).

Oswald Mathias Ungers
(1926-)

German architect. His own house shows simple blocky geometric forms. He was a proponent of Modernism, and the context in which buildings stand, combined with historical references.

Johan Otto von Spreckelsen
(1929-1987)
Danish architect, who used pure forms such as the cylinder and sphere in his work. He was (with Paul Andrew) winner of the competition for the design of the Grande Arche de la D'efense, Paris (1983), which terminates the axis that runs from the Tuileries Gardens in the east through the Arc de Triomphe to La D'efense.

Arata Isozaki
(1931-)
Japanese architect who synthesized western and Japanese themes, concentrating on the clarity of geometry and pure forms as in the Gumma Prefectural Museum of Fine Arts, Takasaki (1974). His recent works include the Museum of Contemporary Art, Los Angeles (1981), and Team Disney Headquarter, Buena Vista, Florida (1990).

Ronald James Herron
(1930-1998)
London-born architect associated with Archigram in the 1960s. His vision for Walking Cities was published widely and is exhibited internationally.

James Stewart Polshek
(1930-)
Most noted for the New York State Bar Center, Albany, (1971), and most recently designer of the new Rose Planetarium at the Museum of Natural History, New York City (2000).

Stanley Tigerman
(1930-)
American architect who opened his office in 1964. The early work was reminiscent of SOM and Mies Van der Rohe, but his growing eclecticism produced many controversial structures.

Aldo Rossi
(1931-1997)
Italian architect and the most eminent protagonist of Rational architecture. His work embraced aspects of International Modernism and a surrealism reminiscent of the paintings of Giorgio de Chirico.

Denise Scott Brown
(1931-)
Zambian-born architect, married Robert Venturi in 1967 and is a partner in Venturi, Rauch & Scott Brown. She influenced Venturi's book, *Learning from Las Vegas* (1972).

Art Moderne (1930-1945)
    Another modern style, it is characterized by soft rounded corners, flat roofs, and with smooth wall finishes without surface ornamentation. It created a distinctive streamlined look, using curved window glass wrapping around corners. Ornamentation consisted of mirrored panels, and cement panels with low relief. Aluminum and stainless steel was used for door and window trim, railings and balusters. Metal or wooden doors often had circular windows.

Peter Eisenman
(1932-)
Founded the Institute of Architecture and Urban Studies in New York City, and was associated with the New York Five from 1972. He is associated with Deconstructivism. His well-known Wexner Center for the Visual Arts, Columbus, Ohio (1883), is set on an angle to the existing campus buildings.

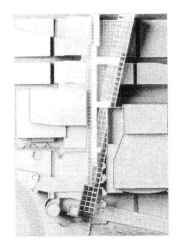

Hugh Gelston Hardy
(1932-)
American architect who formed a partnership with Malcolm Holzman and Norman Pfeiffer in New York City. The firm designed many theaters and became known for its use of disparate parts, seemingly thrown together, giving an impression of incompleteness.

Michael Graves
(1934-)
One of the most controversial American architects. He was identified as one of the New York Five, and first became known for a series of private houses based on reworked themes of Le Corbusier. His work was Post-modern. The Public Services Building, Portland, Oregon (1979), and the Humana Tower, Louisville, Kentucky (1982), are celebrated examples of his work.

Richard Alan Meier
(1934-)
Worked with Marcel Breuer and SOM, and was the most prolific of the New York Five. He persisted in using white in his buildings such as the Saltzman House, East Hampton, New York (1967), and the Douglas House, Harbor Springs, Michigan (1971). His later works include the High Museum of Art, Atlanta, (1980), and the vast Getty Center, Los Angeles (1984).

Sir Norman Robert Foster
(1935-)
English architect, and one of the most distinguished practitioners of the High-Tech style. His largest commissions were the Hong Kong and Shanghai Bank, Hong Kong (1979), Willis Faber U. Dumas Building, Ipswich (1974), and the Hong Kong International Airport, the largest enclosed space in the world (1998).

Donlyn Lyndon
(1936-)
Partner in the firm of Moore, Lyndon, Turnbull in San Francisco.

Renzo Piano
(1937-)
Italian architect, who worked with Richard Rogers designing the High-Tech Pompidou Center, Paris (1971). He was much influenced by Futurism, Constructivism, and Archigram.

John Andrews
(1933-)
Australian-born architect who made his name with Scarborough College, University of Toronto (1964), a megastructure using the raw materials and the chunky forms of New Brutalism. He designed the George Gund Hall, Harvard University, Cambridge (1972). He also designed the CN Tower, Toronto (1975).

Kisho Noriani Kurokawa
(1934-)
Japanese architect and prominent force in Metabolism, where life sciences relate to architecture more than to machine aesthetics. The Nakagin Capsule Tower, Tokyo (1971), was a sophisticated building incorporating the latest technology. His later work includes the gigantic Pacific Tower, La Defense, Paris (1991).

Hans Hollien
(1934-)
Austrian-born architect, who established his reputation with small well-crafted shops, detailed with meticulous care, and in sharp contrast to the surrounding façades. He also designed museums, among them the Museum of Modern Art, Frankfurt (1987).

Imre Makovecz
(1935-)
Hungarian architect influenced by the work of Rudolph Steiner. He designed the Hungarian Pavilion for Expo '92, Seville, Spain, with seven church-like spires rising through the roof.

Peter Cook
(1936-   )
Founder in 1960 of Archigram, consisting of a group of designers who disbanded in 1975. They promoted the High-Tech style through seductive futuristic graphics. His Plug-in City was a matrix of changeable parts inserted into grid-like structures.

Moshe Safde
(1938-)
Israeli-born Canadian architect who designed the Habitat Housing, Montreal, Canada, for Expo '67, which consisted of prefabricated concrete housing units fitted together in an experimental design.

Charles Gwathmey
(1938-)
Identified as one of the New York Five. He formed a partnership in 1971 with Albert Siegal. Most of their early work was private houses. Major other works include the Disney World Convention Center, Orlando (1990) and the Guggenheim Museum expansion, New York City (1991).

Robert Krier
(1938-)
Luxembourg-born Austrian architect, brother of Leon Krier, who built many housing projects in Berlin (1970s). He has been dubbed a devotee of Neo-Rationalism.

Ricardo Bofill Levi
(1939-)
Barcelona-born architect, who designed a series of enormous Post-modern housing blocks such as Les Espaces d'Abraxas, Marne-La-Vallee (1979), near Paris. It is a typical example of his monumental stripped Neo-classical style.

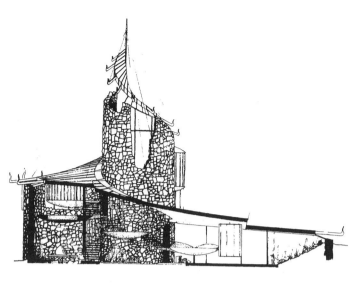

Robert A.M. Stern
(1939-)
Worked with Richard Meier before setting up his own practice in 1977. He is seen as one of the influences in Post-modernism, advocating a study of history and eclectic use of forms.

American School (1940-1959)
The later work of Frank Lloyd Wright and the early work of Bruce Goff are both characteristic of this style. It represents the association of organic principles, such as the relationship of the part to the whole, with the character of self-sufficiency, rejection of tradition, free expression, and passion for the land.

Helmut Jahn
(1940-)
German-born American architect; joined the firm of C.F. Murphy in Chicago, in 1967. Studied with Mies van der Rohe, but his later work moved to a new richness of expression drawing on aspects of Art Deco for a unique expression. In Chicago, designed O'Hare International Airport (1965), the Exhibition Building at McComick Place (1971), Xerox Center (1980), and the State of Illinois Center (1985).

Todao Ando
(1941-)
Internationally recognized, largely self-educated Japanese architect. He founded his office in Osaka. He uses traditional materials, vernacular style, and modern techniques of construction.

Mario Botta
(1943-)
Swiss architect who worked with Le Corbusier and Louis Kahn. Designed a series of private houses in Lugano, Switzerland, which were set alone in the landscape, and the Botta House at Riva San-Vitale (1972), which had strong geometric forms. His late work includes the Museum of Modern Art in San Francisco (1995).

Rem Koohaus
(1944-)
Dutch architect who formed the Office for Metropolitan Architecture (OMA) in 1975, producing a number of visionary and theoretical projects, including *Delirious New York.*, later published as a book (1978). He was a publicist for Deconstructivism.

Bernard Schumi
(1944-)
Swiss-born American architect, one of seven identified with Deconstructivism. His best-known work is the Parc de La Villette, Paris (1984), a series of red toy-like sculptural forms set into the intersection points of a large site grid.

Brutalism (1945-1960)

This term refers to an uncompromisingly modern style which expresses itself in a huge scale in raw and exposed material such as concrete. It emphasized stark forms, and was distinguished by its weight, texture and massiveness, created mainly by large areas of patterned concrete. Windows tend to be tiny holes, and the combination of voids and solids may give walls an egg-crate appearance. Mechanical systems are left exposed on the interior of the bare structure.

Leon Krier
(1946-)

Luxembourg-born architect and theorist, who championed Rational Architecture. His view of the city as a document of intelligence, memory, and pleasure is the antithesis of the concept of the disposable, adaptable, Plug-in City of Archigram and other advocates. He was critical of Postmodernism.

Zaha Hadid
(1950-)

Iraqi architect, trained under Rem Koolhaas and associated with Deconstructivism. Her work is fragmented and jagged, as in the Monsoon Bar, Sapparo, Japan. Other work includes the extensions to the Dutch Parliament Building, the Hague (1978). Most of her designs have remained on paper.

Formalism (1950-1965)

This term represents a trend towards a new classicism in American architecture. It was manifested in buildings by Mies Van der Rohe, Phillip Johnson, Paul Rudolph and Minuro Yamasaki.

Simon Rodilla

Italian-born mason who built an artistic fantasy on the outskirts of Los Angeles, consisting of steel-framed, free-form towers, constructed of concrete-covered reinforcing rods encrusted with inlaid tile, shells, and fragments of broken bottles (1954).

New Brutalism (1953-1965)

This was representative of buildings which expressed the materials, structure and services honestly, in the tradition of Le Corbusier.

Robert Anshen

Partner in the firm of Anshen and Allen, San Francisco, California. Designed the Chapel of the Holy Cross, Sedona, Arizona (1956).

William Caudill

Partner in the firm Caudill, Rowlett, Scott (CRS), most well-known for its style of involving the user groups to participate in the design "charrette" process, from 1958 to 1973.

Welton Becket

Head of his successful Los Angeles architectural firm. Designed the Hyatt Regency Hotel and Reunion Tower, Dallas (1978), and the Kaiser Center, Oakland (1960), and numerous office buildings.

Archigram
(1960-1975)

Group formed by Peter Cook, Ron Herron, Dennis Crompton, and others, who published their ideas through seductive graphics, exhibitions, and the magazine *Archigram*.

Modernism (1960-1975)

This term comes from the Latin *modo*, meaning "just now." Every successive style is theoretically modern until superseded by the next. Revival styles can be built with modern materials and techniques. The Modern Movement was the conscious attempt to find an architecture tailored to modern life and one that made use of new materials. It rejected the concept of applied style and the use of ornament.

Neo Expressionism (1964-1975)

Structures which express continuity of form by sweeping curves characterize this style. These structures were primarily the result of using reinforced concrete to create smooth shapes and seamless soaring forms.

Neo Formalism (1964-1970)

A style which combines the classical symmetrical forms and smooth wall surfaces with arches of precast concrete and decorative metal grilles, often delicate in appearance.

Contextualism (1960-1970)

An approach to urban planning that considers the city in its totality, is the view that the experience of a city is greater than the sum of its parts. According to proponents, architecture must fit in, respond to, and mediate its surroundings.

Pop Architecture (1962-1974)

A style which refers to buildings that are popular with a large section of the public, or structures that symbolically represent objects, fantastic designs for vast sculptures on an architectural scale, or any architecture produced more as idea than building.

Plug-in (1964-1970)

The group Archigram proposed this new type of architecture. It consisted of a basic structure to contain transportation and communication services and a series of separate units; domestic environments, shops, and leisure activities, that are plugged in.

John Graham

Designed the Space Needle at the Science Center, Seattle (1962).

Megastructures (1964-1976)

Vast new structures were proposed by a number of architects to replace existing cities. In the design of megastructures, individual buildings become merely components, or lose their individuality altogether. Their overall purpose is to provide a total environment for work and leisure.

Charles Luckman
Partner with William Periera in the firm of Periera and Luckman. They designed the space-age restaurant at the Los Angeles International Airport.

Max Urbahn
Designed the Vehicle Assembly Building at the JFK Space Center, Cape Canaveral, Florida (1966).

Antoine Predock
New Mexico-based architect using stark, abstract forms and natural desert materials.

Biotecture (1966-1970)
A term combining "biology" and "architecture." was coined by Rudolph Doernach. It denotes architecture as an artificial "super system" as live, dynamic, and mobile.

Pneumatic (1967-1993)
This term refers to inflatable structures, air inflated, air supported, and air controlled. Structures generally consist of curved forms, domes or half cylinders.

Environmental Design (1970-)
Scientific design and control of the man-made environment defines this style. Its concern is with the total environment, encompassing topics such as architecture, urban planning, engineering, lighting, heating acoustics, and ergonomics.

Shipporeit-Heinrich
Originally from the office of Mies van der Rohe, G.D. Shipporeit and John C. Heinrich designed the first skyscraper entirely enclosed in glass, the Lake Point Towers, Chicago (1968).

SITE (Sculpture in the Environment)
American group launched by James Wines, and best known for the Best Products chain of stores, where unique manipulation of architectural elements made the buildings notorious. One of the most unique, but never realized, was the "highrise of houses", wherein a neighborhood of complete single-story residences were stacked within a steel superstructure. The later work includes the exhibits at Expo '92, Seville, Spain (1992).

Ecological (1970-)
In response to the problems of expensive fuels, various projects were undertaken to construct self-sufficient, self-serving buildings. They are independent of public utilities by exploiting ambient energy sources such as wind power and solar radiation, and by recycling techniques.

Ersatz (1973-1975)
This German word means "substitute" or "replacement". Architectural critic Charles Jencks has used this term to describe architecture with forms borrowed indiscriminately from various sources. This is partly the result of modern technology, which is capable of producing architecture in any style. It can also be considered as any "pastiche" which captures the essence of the original.

Edward Larrabee Barnes
His most noted early work is the Crown Center, Kansas City (1968). Later works include the IBM Building, New York City (1983), and the Walker Art Center, Minneapolis (1971).

Formalism (1970-1976)
This theory assigns priority to the form at the expense of all its other characteristics. It is possible to discuss the form (shape, structure, pattern, organization of part to whole), and the content (substance, subject) as if they were not inter-dependent.

Kinetic (1971-1985)
A building form which is dynamic, adaptable and responsive to the changing demands of the users depicts this style. The broad category includes a number of other concepts., such as Mobile, Reversible and Deformable architecture. Mobile architecture would not be constantly moving, only capable of being moved if required.

Arcology (1969-)

A conception of architecture involving a fusion of architecture and ecology, was proposed by Paolo Soleri, an Italian architect in America. Arcology is Soleri's solution to urban problems. He proposes vast vertical megastructures capable of housing millions of inhabitants.

Postmodernisnm (1980-)

A reaction against the International style and Modernism was evidenced in this style. It reintroduced ornament and decorative motifs to building design, often in garish colors and illogical juxtaposition. It is an eclectic borrowing of historical details from several periods, but unlike previous revivals, is not concerned with scholarly reproduction. Instead it is a light-hearted compilation of aesthetic symbols and details, often using arbitrary geometry, and with an intentional inconsistency of scale. The most prevalent aspect is the use of irony, ambiguity, and contradiction in the use of architectural forms. Those connected with the beginning of this movement include Aldo Rossi, Stanley Tigerman, Charles Moore, and Michael Graves.

The Architects Collaborative (TAC)

A firm started by Walter Gropius in Cambridge. They designed the American Institute of Architects National Headquarters Building, Washington, DC (1973).

John Hejduk

One of the original New York Five, and dean of the Cooper Union School of Architecture, which he renovated (1974).

Eugene Kohn

Partner in the firm Kohn, Pederson, Fox, with William Pederson and Sheldon Fox. They designed the Proctor and Gamble General Offices, Cincinnati (1985), and 333 Wacker Drive, Chicago (1983), among many other office structures.

Morphosis

A California firm of architects led by Thom Mayne (1944-) and Michael Rotondi (1949-) whose aim is to absorb the idiosyncratic by drawing on the more terrifying aspects of technology. Their Venice, California, house has a system of weights and pulleys controlling sun-sails that change the appearance of the building.

Arquitectonica

High-style designers in the Post-modern style. The Atlantis apartments in Miami (1982) was their first major work. Their latest is the e-walk apartment and commercial development in Times Square, New York City (2000).

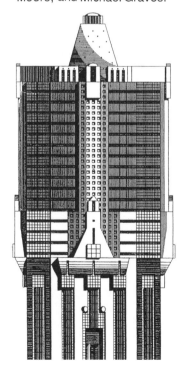

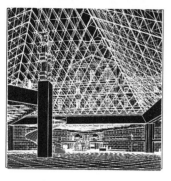

New Classicism (1982-)

The final phase of Post-Modernism has led to a new form of Classicism, a free-style version of the traditional language. It shares traditional assumptions of previous revivals, such as relating ideas to the past and using universal figures of representation as the design vocabulary. It combines two purist styles - Classicism and Modernism - and adds new forms based on new technologies and social usage. Previous rules of composition are not disregarded, but extended and distorted. Among those identified with this style are James Stirling, Robert Venturi, Michael Graves, Hans Hollein, Charles Moore and Arata Isozaki.

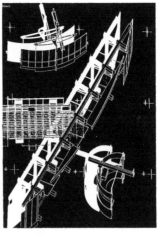

Deconstruction (1984-)

This style is known as a "Neo-Modern" architecture or "Post-Structuralism," and takes many of its forms from the work of the Constructivists of the 1920's, such as Tchernikhov and Leonidou. It takes modernist abstraction to an extreme and exaggerates already known motifs. It is an anti-social architecture, based on intellectual abstraction. Some of its proponents are Bernard Tschumi and his design for the Parc de la Villette, Paris; Peter Eisenman's Wexner Center for the Visual Arts, Ohio; and work by Frank Gehry, SITE, Architectonica, and Morphosis.

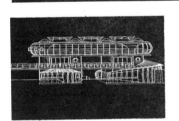

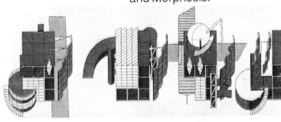

Organic (1985)

There are two styles which have reoccured throughout history in different forms and expressions - classicism and it's opposite force, the organic style. The historicism of the former is matched by the expression of personal freedom of the latter.

The organic principles rely on the integration of form and function. The structure and appearance of the building is based on a unity of forms that relate to the natural environment in a deliberate way. It also stresses the integration of individual parts to the whole concept, and that all forms should express the natural use of materials.

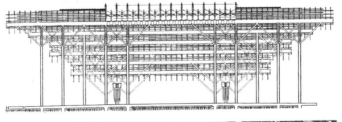

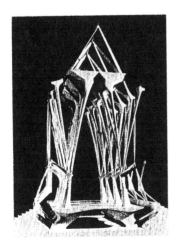

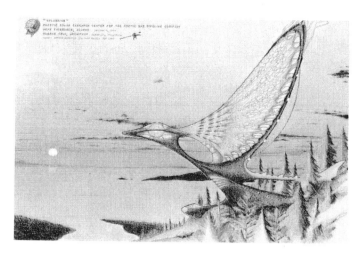

Evolutionary (1990-)

Defined by its major proponent, Eugene Tsui, as design that grows and develops based on climatic and ecological elements, as well as advances in science and technology. The design is approached as a living organism as if natural forces had shaped the structure.

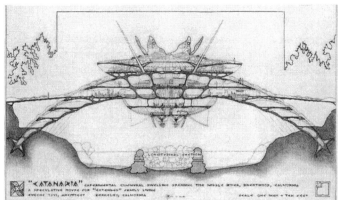

Conceptual

This form of architecture is also called "invisible" and "imaginary" architecture, since it represented plans and drawings for buildings and cities that have never been constructed. These can legitimately be regarded as architecture arrested at the conceptual stage of development.

"Simulated" architecture would consist of holographic images of monuments projected into space by laser beams. "Invisible" architecture would represent an expenditure of energy to create walls and furniture by the use of jets of air instead of conventional building materials, and allow for instant buildings.

Conceptual architecture has also been defined as a limitless activity devoid of direction or dogma; that is, pure research or speculation. It could also be applied to work which could be realized but lacked the funds to construct it, or work which was done as an end in itself.

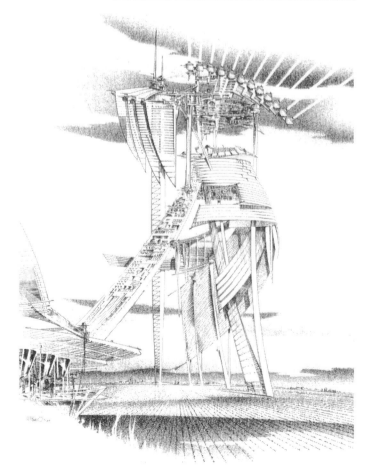

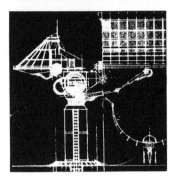

A work of architecture is not just a structure built by and for certain people at a particular time and in a characteristic style. Nor is it built only to fulfill a given utilitarian or symbolic function. It is also an art form. The architect uses a variety of design tools to achieve the desired balance of functional concerns and beauty of form. Although all buildings that exist have been classified in a particular style and tradition, the basic aesthetic considerations that brought them into being have always been the same.

To design means to create. It involves associating and arranging forms into new meanings. The invention and disposition of forms, elements, and materials according to a plan, which represents a myriad of functional and economic constraints, is designing a building. A building represents something, it embodies an attitude of the person or society who built it. Many buildings have a symbolic function. The Byzantine church is a representation of heaven on earth; the layout of a Hindu temple is a symbolic world map. The Egyptian dwelling was a temporary lodging, while the tomb was a permanent home. A building does not express its meaning in the same manner as a painting or piece of sculpture, because it is much more complex by nature.

Buildings are designed conceptually from plan and sectional views, and developed through elevations and perspective sketches and finally in three-dimensional models or computer-generated walk-through images. We can never see a building in its totality the way the designer was able to see it, and we can never get more than a partial view of the exterior or interior. There are certain major architectural qualities of mass and above all of space that are only discovered on physical inspection. As we approach a structure, it changes in appearance (aspect), and as we examine it in more detail, often with the aid of plans and sections, we expect to discover more the closer we look. We expect to see the most obscure and smallest elements worked out in terms of the overall concept, to be a special part of that pattern of form. Prejudices are meaningless in the discussion of architecture because each idea and form, regardless of time or place, has value to the vocabulary of design.

The design process involves a series of decisions, taken one at a time. Decisions narrow choices, until there is usually only one optimum solution. It begins with defining the project, determining the scope, site and budget limitations. Next is the analysis of design approaches. A definition of the specifics follows, which involves concrete decisions about form, structure and materials. This is followed by an examination of alternatives, which limits the design options. Next, a selection of specific characteristics comes from our own reservoir of talent and expertise. Finally, there is a clarification and critical appraisal which reviews all the design decisions involved in the process.

Whenever a designer puts pencil to paper, (or mouse to screen), questions are raised about space, enclosure, geometric organization, the treatment of surfaces and the use of materials. What the final physical structure must express is the aesthetic attitude as well as the technological and social ones. There are many practical considerations as well in the discussion of the design of any building. Many factors affect the way a building is constructed. These include climate, geophysical influences and availability of materials. The final two factors are the client or user and the builder.

During the Middle Ages craftspeople and artisans were involved in every project, and although the names are known of a few of the early Egyptian and Greek architects, it was not until the Renaissance that buildings were clearly attributed to the architects, who wore many other hats as well. They were painters, sculptors, mathematicians, engineers, scientists and theorists. And then there were the patrons who commissioned the work. In the past the greatest patrons were kings, the wealthy class, and religious powers. Today the architect must work with corporate clients, governmental agencies, planning commissions and other public authorities. All these factors impact on the final architectural design.

The most important issue to the designer is how to gather and simulate all these influences and constraints and design a project using a wide vocabulary of design considerations and creative forms for expression of his or her ideas. The main fact is that architecture takes on meaning in relation to people. Therefore, its easy to see why Renaissance architects based their design theories on the humanistic ideals of ancient Greece, and related the basic units of measurement (scale) to human figures (proportion). At other times, especially in Rome, architecture was designed to produce a sense of awe, a superhuman scale (monumentality). Architects in classical antiquity had little sense of the true dynamics of design elements. They emphasized horizontal moldings dividing the stories, while the cornice defined the sky. By adjusting the horizontal and vertical members (articulation), by moving them closer together or further apart, by giving them different emphasis, interesting and varied patterns (rhythms) were obtained.

Architects from the Renaissance onwards have explored these possibilities using the classical system of pilasters, columns and entablatures in all manner of combinations, developing numerous kinds of bay units and intermixing the classical orders. The new forms cut through the entablature and extended to the roof, creating a totally new effect. Space and light are products of the volumes and surfaces of the building itself. At the same time the surfaces can be enlivened and given more movement with sculptural forms, by the play of curves or diagonals, and by the use of contrasting textures and colors. The architect has an inexhaustible variety of materials at his or her disposal today whereby natural textures can be used in creative combination with other manufactured products.

Volumes and facades determine the external appearance of a building. It remains to discover what is enclosed behind the walls, the interior space that is unique to architecture. The architect works with space as well as solid walls, and the balance between solid and void is the most basic consideration. On the outside there is a choice to make in the transition from solid to void (modulation) and whether it will be abrupt or gradual. This is where the interplay of various design ideas acts in a combined expression. Not only should a building have a consistency from the interior to the exterior, but in a broader concern it should be related to its surroundings in one manner or another. The siting of a building or complex should be as carefully considered as the structure itself. Streets and squares are open-air spaces enclosed by buildings in much the same way as interior spaces. So it is important that every aspect of the project is related to the identical design concept.

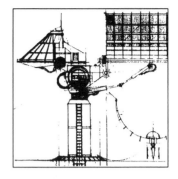

Composition:

A putting together of parts or elements to form a whole, or the manner in which such parts are combined or related to form a unified whole.
(from Latin composito, from componere; to put together.)

Articulation
To unite by forming a joint or joints, or to divide into joints; the method or manner of joining surfaces together to define a form. From the Greek "articulus" meaning small joint.

Related definitions are;

Attachment; *act of joining.*

Combination: *junction to produce a whole.*

Incorporation: *a mixture of elements*

Junction: *the line or point where two things are joined or hinged.*

Link: *part of a connected series.*

Meeting: *a coming together.*

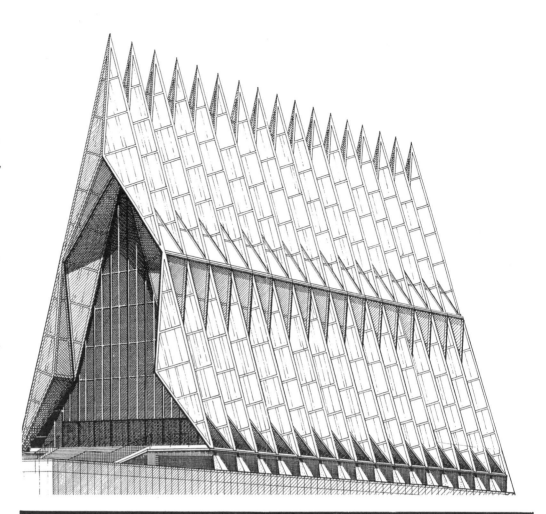

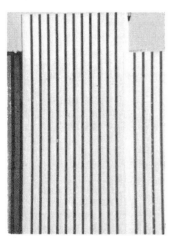

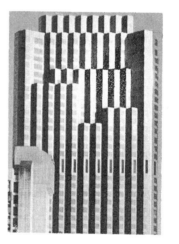

Aspect

The point from which one looks, a point of view; a position facing a given direction, an exposure.

Aspect changes as we move closer or farther away from a building or group of buildings. Aspect also applies to the way we see a building in terms of forms or differences in light and shade on entire surfaces or on details.

Asymmetry

Not symmetrical, with the parts not arranged correspondingly identical on both sides of a central axis.

It creates a sense of equilibrium by the arrangement of two sets of forms of different size and shape on either side of an imaginary axis, so that they appear to be equal in weight or importance. This is

Axis

An imaginary straight line about which parts of a building or a group of buildings can be arranged.

The axis may be made visible through the use of forms or materials, or it might be invisible and defined mainly by the space and volume. The elements can be arranged either in a symmetrical or asymmetrical manner.

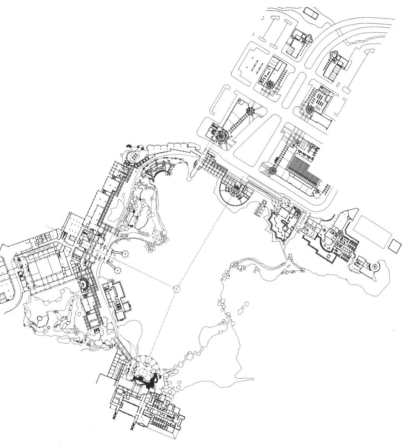

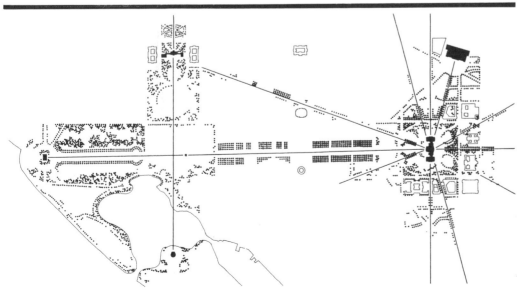

Balance

Indicates a harmonizing or satis-fying arrangement, or propor-tion of parts or elements, as in a design or composition; the state of equi-poise between different elements.

Formal: *characterized by all symmetrical elements.*

Informal balance: *means the forms are asymmetrical.*

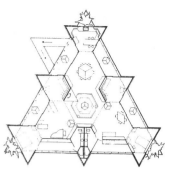

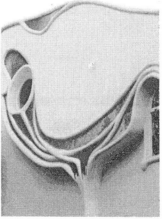

Blending

A gradual merging of one thing into another; the process of bringing together into one.

Related definitions include:

Incorporation: *a mixture of elements.*

Unification: *the process of bringing together into one.*

Union: *a seamless junction of parts.*

Chiaroscuro

The effect of light and shadow within an area or composition, brought about by the use of deep variations to enhance the architectural forms.

Light and shadow is the means by which we perceive architectural form. Sunlight is the dynamic source that defines the character that the designer intended, as it heightens the contours of moldings and joints of the materials through shadows. Sunlight is also a scale shaping element. It can add definition to the forms and affect the qualities of scale of the building.

Geographic and climatic considerations may require adjustments in the design of details to compensate for the amount of light to produce sufficient shadows. The most notable example is the difference between Renaissance and Gothic detailing in England versus those in Italy where sunlight was stronger.

Shadows are a shifting form of darkness, and have been used since the earliest cultures to highlight sculptural forms incised into the material, and to define the shape and rhythm of ornamental details.

Climax:

A number of ideas so arranged that each succeeding one raises above its predecessor in force. The culmination or highest point is the summation of the whole process, the point of greatest intensity.

Color

A dye, pigment, paint or other substance that imparts receptors to the eye in terms of dominant wavelength, luminance, hue, and brightness.

The creative use of color can be achieved through the use of a mix of natural materials. Stone and brick can be used in contrasting ways, usually by banding. Many modern materials can be combined to produce interesting patterns and textures.

Color in the built environment generally has a more subtle effect on people than other building elements. The whiteness of Greek structures may have symbolized purity, whereas the terra-cotta color of unadorned brick shows the earthiness of the clay from which it was formed.

Complexity

Consisting of various parts united or connected together, formed by a combination of different elements; intricate, interconnecting parts that are not easily disentangled.

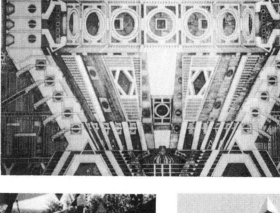

Composition

The forming by a combination of various elements, putting things into proper position to form a whole in terms of the structure or organization.

Contextual

Any doctrine emphasizing the importance of the context in establishing the meaning of terms.

The setting into which a building is placed, its site, its natural environment, or its neighborhood is considered its context. A structure can echo its neighbors' colors or contrast its massiveness with delicacy. Some of the elements that contribute to the context are building heights, proportions of the facades, rhythms of solids to voids, relation of one building to the next, and the patterns of each. The repetition of colors or building materials add to the continuity of the street.

Other constructed elements that are considered part of the context include landscaping, street furniture, paving, park benches, kiosks, and signage.

Contrast

To show differences of form or color , or to set in opposition in order to emphasize the differences.

The quality of opposition of line, form or materials can form contrasts. Elements of differing character that are placed next to each other or in the immediate vicinity can form contrasts. The purpose is to make one element or form stand out more sharply when used against or in combination with another.

Counterpoint
A contrasting but parallel element or theme.

In parallel counterpoint, the ideas run together, but do not cross or interweave, just like bands along the same direction. In overlapping counterpoint, the forms are in contact but do not connect. In interweaving counterpoint the forms or elements are integrated, with each being a part of the other.

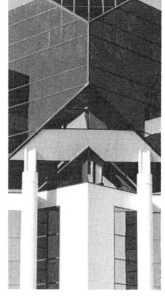

Depth
The extent, measurement or distance from top to bottom (downwards), or from front to back (inwards), or something consisting of several layers.

Depth is not only a matter of thickness. It can be achieved by the proper spatial relationships of elements, and by "concealing" from view the whole space at one time. Depth can be achieved by receding, overlapping, and interweaving planes. Color and texture can create the illusion of depth by being able to see into it. Depth can be created by the use of chiaroscuro (light and shadow). by transparency (see through it), by translucency (see into it), by reflection (adding another dimension), and by perforations (seeing through to beyond).

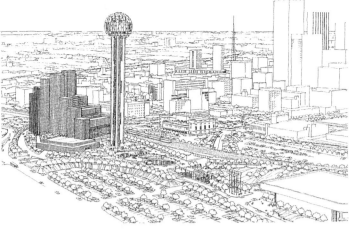

Dominance
Occupying a preeminent or most influential position; exercising the most influence or governing control.

Emphasis
A special importance or significance placed upon or imparted to something; a sharpness or vividness of outline.

Emphasis requires that one idea or design theme be dominant, and is important in achieving unity in design. The idea that dominates is given greater forcefulness through the purposeful subordination of lesser important elements or features.

Focus
A center of interest or activity drawing attention to the most important aspect of a design scheme, such as the main space, scale, materials, lighting, or orientation.

Form

The contour and structure of an object as distinguished from its substance or from the matter composing it; its distinctive appearance as determined by its visible lines.

Related definitions include:

Configuration: *A pattern comprising an outline together with a detailed arrangement of parts within the outline. An external shape.*

Contour: *The boundary lines of a three-dimensional or solid figure.*

Formal: *Having to do with the form or shape as opposed to the content.*

Outline: *Defines the outer limits, giving it a two-dimensional representation.*

Profile: *Denotes the outline of the human face, or any other shape, in a side view. Any distinctive outline.*

Shape: *Implies a three-dimensional definition that indicates outline and bulk.*

Size: *Defines all the actual dimensions in terms of length, width and depth.*

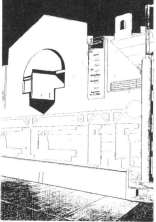

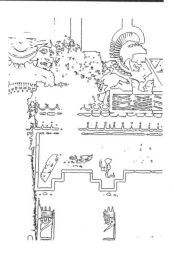

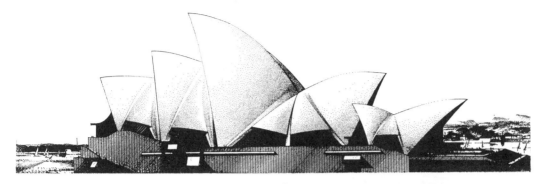

Regardless of the materials, architectural forms are distributed in families that stem from geometric figures to free forms; curved forms are most characterized by the sphere, triangular forms includes all planes, polygons, and solids, and free forms include everything else. In architectural design it is important to have a wide vocabulary of forms without any prejudices. Then the whole range of forms, from geometric to free forms, will be available to use as the situation calls for.

The main categories of architectural form includes external forms and internal forms. Resultant forms occur where the two come together.

Harmonic Proportions
Relates the consonances of the musical scale to those of architectural design, particularly to theories of proportion.

Classical Greek theories related music to geometry, and was repeated in the Renaissance especially by Alberti and Palladio. They believed that architecture was based on mathematics, expressing the harmonic structure exhibited by other natural laws.

Harmony
The pleasing interaction or appropriate combination of the elements in a whole.

Related definitions include:

Compatible: *A capacity for existing together without discord.*

Congruous: *Suggests a fitness or an appropriateness of component parts .*

Consistent: *Implies such agreement between details of the same thing or between related things that they will not be in conflict.*

Consonant: *Shows harmony between two things.*

Hierarchy
An arrangement or system of ranking one above the other or arranged in a graded series or sequence such as size (large to small), shape (similar or dissimilar), and placement (emphasis or location).

Incident:
Subordinate to the whole scheme, but is used to give points of reference along the way and to create interest.

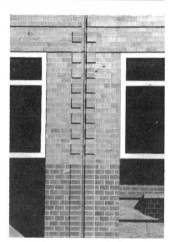

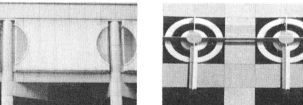

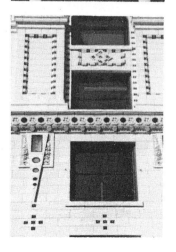

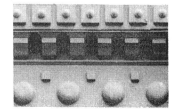

Light
A source of illumination such as the sun or electric lamp, as perceived by the human eye.

Light is one of the most powerful external elements in defining architectural form. It can expand space or reduce the effect of mass. It can change color and texture.

Natural light changes with the time of day, the seasons, weather conditions, orientation of the building and geographic location. Artificial light is controllable and can be used to counteract the effects of natural light. Although used primarily on interior spaces, it is often used on the exterior for dramatic night lighting.

Line
A line is the path of a point extended through space; it may be geometric (straight lines and arcs), free form (flowing and curving), or a combination of the two.

A line, theoretically considered and defined, is the result of projecting a point in a given direction. It may be long or short, broad or narrow. Lines may vary in direction. If they change gradually they become curved. If they change abruptly they become angular. The line may combine both of these characteristics and assume shapes of infinite variety. A wavy line is formed by a succession of undulating or elongated "S" curves.

A series of small points set closely together can simulate a line, or can be considered as a dotted or broken line. We can also use a line as a solo element, or to enclose an area. A line has its own character, as it can be generated from any shape or cross section (point). It can be straight, curved or free-form, and influences the outside space as well as the shape of the object it encloses. Lines can be thick or thin, they can swell or taper or have uniform thickness, and they can be smooth or jagged.

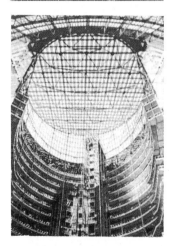

Mass

The physical volume or bulk of a solid body, or a grouping of individual parts or elements that compose a unified body of unspecified size.

The same qualities that apply to shape apply to mass. The mass of a structure can often approach monumentality if it is impressively large or without elements of human scale.

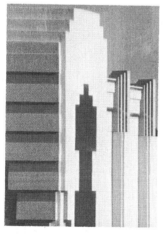

Modulation
To measure, to adjust to, or regulate by a certain proportion; to temper or to soften in passing from one element , form, or material to another.

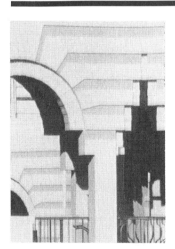

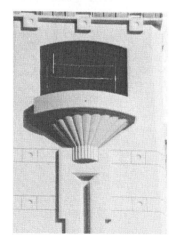

Module

A unit that is characteristic of a program or design, and used as a standard unit for measuring.

In antiquity all architecture was strictly modular. The best examples are the "orders" of Greece and Rome. The module chosen as the basis for all buildings was the radius of the column, not some external element in space. Since each module was unique for that order, each building was different in size, but belonged to the same modular order.

The Japanese used a modular unit based on their tatami mat, and the dimensions of rooms and all structural elements are exact multiples of this modular unit.

A module can represent a standard unit of measurement, to which all other items are proportional. For example in "modular" construction the module is not a unit of proportion, but a standard size used for coordinating the dimensions of building components (doors, windows, panels and beams), with the dimensions of the openings in a projected building into which they are intended to fit.

The "modulor" was a system of proportion developed by Le Corbusier in 1942, which was based on the theories of early civilizations, and on the human form. The system was related to the golden section.

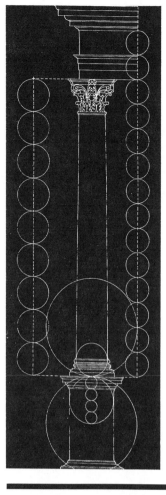

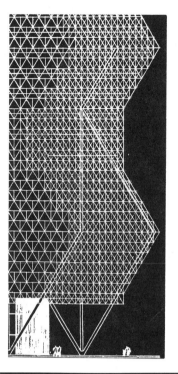

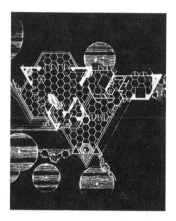

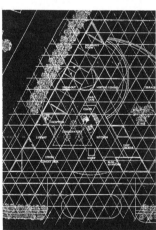

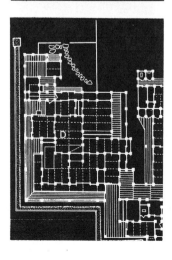

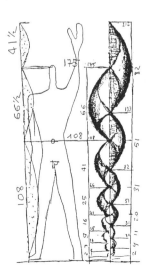

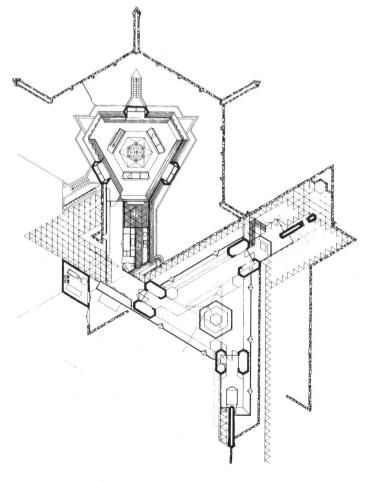

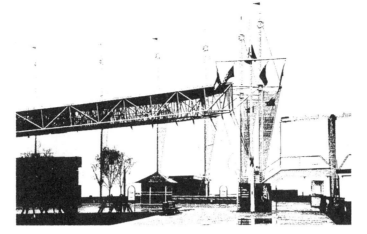

Orchestration
To combine harmoniously.

In architecture, the materials are orchestrated, rather than musical instruments. Each have their own color and texture, and it makes a difference how they are coordinated to harmonize and work together. The character of each material must be in character with the rest. The result must feel so right that no other combination of materials would suffice.

Order

A logical and regular arrangement among the separate components or elements of a group; a unity of idea, feeling and form.

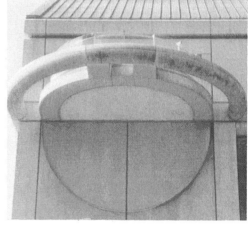

Orientation
The placement of a structure on a site with regard to local conditions of sunlight, wind and drainage, and vistas.

Ornamentation
Any adjunct or detail used to adorn, decorate, or embellish the appearance or add to the general aesthetic effect.

Related definitions include:

Ornament: *Every detail, shape, texture and color that is deliberately exploited or added to attract an observer, or to enhance the surface.*

Ornate: *Excessively detailed.*

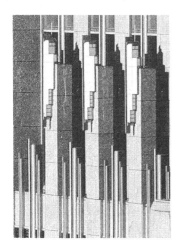

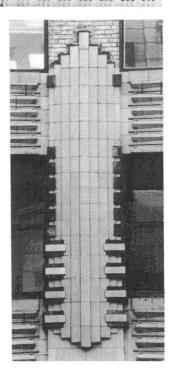

Pattern
The juxtaposition of repetitive elements in a design.

The ordered arrangement of parts into a pattern may occur at various scales and different patterns are obvious at different distances. Small-scale patterns created by individual units contrast with large-scale patterns created by entire wall sections on facades.

On the outside of a building the placement of columns, arches, carvings, balconies and slabs creates patterns, as any break in the plane surface catches light and casts shadows, creating patterns.

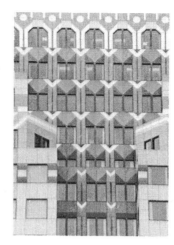

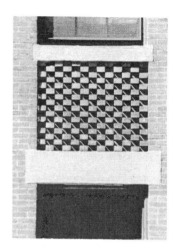

Plane

The simplest kind of two-dimensional surface, defined by its length and width.

The fundamental property of a plane is its shape and surface characteristics. The three-dimensional volumes of forms and mass are defined by the various planes and their relationships.

For example, the horizontal ground plane is the one on which the structure sits, the vertical planes define the shape of the structure, and a top plane defines the roof. The primary vertical frontal plane, or "facade" represents the meeting of external factors such as weather and climate, with the internal factors of function and volume.

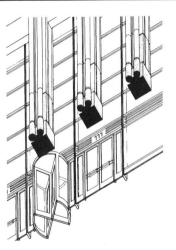

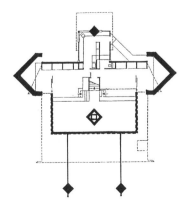
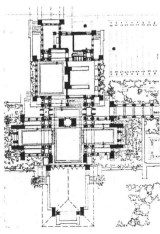
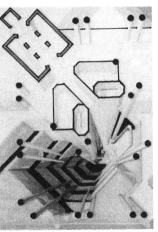

Point

The smallest unit in a composition, depending on the scale of the work; it may be all geometric (straight lines and arcs), free form (flowing and curvilinear), or a combination of each.

Points of any shape can be used repeatedly to form broken or dotted lines, and they can be grouped to form an area of any size.

The extrusion of a point through space results in a line or solid volume, which carries the characteristic shape of the point expressed in its' outline.

Progression

A gradual increase in the size or shape of a form or design keeping the same basic theme or idea.

Proportion

The ratio of one part to another, or its relationship to the whole; a comparative part as to size.

The unit of measure that allowed humans to relate to the things around them were found in the dimensions of their own bodies, a constant and immediate system of reference. Thus many units of measurement are linked very closely to human scale.

Reflection

Action on the part of surfaces, of throwing back rays of light falling upon them.

This reflected image can be used intentionally to complete the visual appearance of any form or pattern. Building materials are selected for their reflective properties, either as low reflectance to focus on the material itself, or for high reflectance to make the building less visible by reflecting its environment or neighbors.

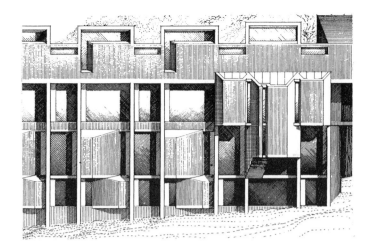

Repitition
The recurrance of rhythmic patterns, forms or accents separated by spaces or different patterns or forms.

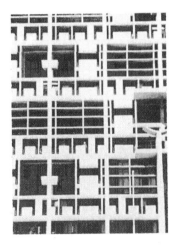

Rhythm
Any kind of movement characterized by the regular occurrence of elements, lines, shapes and forms.; the flow of movement which is shown by light and heavy accents, similar to recurring musical beats.

The three kinds of rhythm include regular (steady or uniform and without variation), irregular (changeable rhythmic flow lacking uniformity), and rhythmic counterpoint (a counter rhythm added to a given rhythm).

Scale

The relationship of one part or the whole of an object to an outside measure, such as the human body.

Proportion and scale are closely associated principles of design. Both deal with the relative size of things. Proportion deals with size relationship within a composition, and scale deals with the size compared to something else, such as the human body. How the elements relate to each other and to their human viewers determines if the scale of a buildings is intimate and in scale with the human (personal scale), or impressively large and out of touch with the human (monumental scale), or if it makes us feel much larger and more significant in relationship to it (diminutive scale).

Simplicity

Characterized by only one aspect, not combined or compounded; without additions or modifications, bare; without embellishment, not ornate, elaborate or adorned.

Related definitions include:

Austere: *Rigorous, unadorned, strict, severely simple.*

Clarity: *Distinct, free from anything which encumbers.*

Plain: *Without ornament or embellishment.*

Pure: *Separate from all extraneous matter. Absolute and clean.*

Simplicity and complexity are not necessarily design opposites, but part of the same idea. Whereas complexity consists of interconnected or interwoven parts, involved or intricate elements, if they are held together with an organizing concept they can become a simple statement.

Site relationship

The plot of land where something was, is, or will be located; the situation or position of a place, town, or building, especially with reference to the surrounding locality.

One of the most important design considerations outside of the building itself is its relationship to the environment, whether urban or suburban. Blending with the site can be restrained to the point of appearing camouflaged.It can relate through smooth modulation. It can employ repetition of textures and colors of the site or surroundings. Contrasting with the site can occur through the use of contrary materials, forms, or through abrupt modulation with the site.

Space

The unlimited continuous three-dimensional expanse in which all material objects exist and all events occur; all of the area in and around a structure, or the volume between specified boundaries, and the interval or linear distance between two points or objects.

The design and control of space relates to the relationship of open areas, both exterior and interior, to the mass of the building. We do not become aware of space until it has been demarcated by forms and shapes.

Symmetry

The exact correspondence of form on opposite sides of a dividing line or plane about the center line or axis.

The types of symmetry are:

Bilateral: *a balanced arrangement of identical similar elements about a central axis.*

Radial: *Consists of balanced elements that radiate from a central point.*

Asymmetry means not symmetrical, but does not imply an unbalance or instability. It is just a different arrangement of elements that have an axis off the center line of the composition, while maintaining balance.

Texture

The representation of the structure of a surface as distinct from color or form, such as showing a grainy, coarse, or dimensional quality as opposed to a uniformly flat, smooth aspect.

The texture of building materials create a wide variety of design effects, from the coldness of marble to the warmth of wood, the roughness of concrete and the smoothness of glass. Materials can also translate a sense of richness or plainness.

Glass can partially reflect the outdoors, mirror it totally or bring it inside through transparency. Concrete, used naturally, creates a solid enduring effect. Stone can be used either smooth, rough, or polished, and wood can organically relate a structure to the natural surroundings.

Visual textures depends on the effect of light and shadow. An awareness of surface characteristics increases with the closeness of the observer. From a distance, pattern may appear as texture, and there is an interaction between the two. Texture depends not only on the surface of the material itself, but on its jointing.

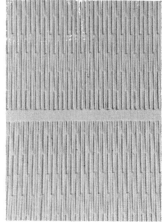

Transformation

The metamorphosis that occurs where primary shapes and forms are changed into other additive or subtractive shapes and forms.

The primary forms are the circle, triangle and square. These are expressed in three-dimensional form as the sphere, cylinder and cone (circles), the cube (square), and the pyramid (triangles). Transformation alters each of these forms within its category.

Translucency

The quality of a material that transmits light sufficiently diffused to eliminate any perception of distinct images beyond.

Transparency

The quality of a material that is capable of transmitting light so that objects or images can be seen as if there were no intervening material, or of such fine open texture that objects may easily be seen on the other side.

Trompe L'oeil
The phrase means "that which deceives the eye."

The phrase was originally used to describe precisely rendered views of earlier centuries, where painters had developed techniques that produced a convincing illusion of reality. This techniques was applied to exterior and interior mural design where elements and even entire architectural facades were painted on blank walls of buildings, thus indicating a particular style, period or design.

Unity
A oneness and absence of diversity; a combination or arrangement of parts and the ordering of all the elements in a work so that each contributes to a total aesthetic effect.

Related definitions include:

Homogeneity: *Involves oneness in the sense of uniformity of overall structure, resulting from a compatibility of components. A totality of related parts*

Integrity: *That unity which indicates the inter-dependence and the completeness of the parts by repetition of module, motif, shape, pattern or size, and harmony of color, texture and materials.*

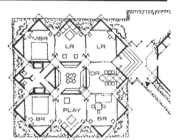

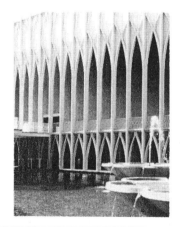

Vernacular
Native or peculiar to a particular country or locality; an architecture concerned with ordinary domestic and functional buildings rather than the essentially monumental.
A form of building based on regional forms and materials.

Volume
The size or extent of any three-dimensional object or region of space; the bulk, size or dimension of a solid body or space.

In early civilizations local materials were almost always the only ones available, and they influenced all succeeding styles. The basic early building materials were wood, reeds and thatching, stone of many varieties, sun-dried and kiln-fired brick. Later, concrete and cement were made from crushed stone, sand and rubble bound with lime. Mud and brick buildings had massive, thick walls with small openings for doors and windows, and these forms were carried over into monumental stone architecture. In Persia and Mesopotamia, where there is a great shortage of building stone, brick construction remained the norm, but from earliest times the brickwork was covered with a facing of stone or ceramic tiles both for decoration and for greater durability. Tiled buildings from Spain to India has their origins in the mud-brick cities of ancient Mesopotamia.

Stone is one of the oldest building materials. The earliest form of stonework was probably rock-cut, generally the enlargement of an existing cave to form an interior space. Early stone huts were made by gathering fieldstone, which cleared the land at the same time. Round stone huts similar to early timber huts occurred throughout the world. Later still, buildings were erected of rough stone, which was then carved in place as if it were natural rock. Throughout history, the stone buildings of dying or conquered civilizations became the convenient raw material for the following period. The Romans pilfered the Etruscans and so on down the line. Dressed stone was an inherent part of Palladian architecture, not only in Renaissance Europe but also in England and America. Classical mansions in the popular revival styles relied heavily on stonework. All the early cultures quarried stone for their monuments, and Gothic architecture made use of small carved stone units to achieve the soaring monumental but still gravity-based structures.

When wood was used, the post-and-lintel was the normal method of construction, and this was carried over even when other materials came along to replace the wooden prototypes. The typical form of a Greek temple reproduces in stone what was originally a wooden structure, and even much of the formal detailing seem to be derived from the wooden model. In China and Japan wood remained the normal building material, except for fortifications, and post-and-lintel construction was elaborated into a complex system of brackets to support the roof.

Each material possesses its own particular design language, which is the expression of its structure. Other factors are its texture and its finish. There are five basic families of materials: rock material, consisting of stone and clay, which is found in a natural state in the ground; organic material, such as the species of wood; metal materials, which are manufactured into refined products such as steel and aluminum, copper and other alloys; synthetic materials, including glass and plastics; and hybrid materials, such as reinforced concrete and other combinations of two or more materials.

Each building material has its own appropriate scale. Brick is a modular masonry unit small enough to be picked up by one hand. Concrete block is larger, most often picked up by two hands. The color and texture of wood provides familiar patterns and textures that relate to a human scale, no matter how large the piece of wood is. Concrete has great flexibility and variety and can produce graceful sculptural forms. The relatively small size of precast concrete panels relate to human scale. Exposed steel construction shows the membering that provides scale. Of course, when different materials are used in the same structure, the scalar qualities change. They interact and reinforce one another and can either blend or contrast.

Reinforced concrete is an artificial monolithic material derived from combining steel and concrete. It is as solid as stone, relatively elastic, flexible and economical to produce. It is self-finishing, speedily erected and fireproof. The use of reinforced concrete construction in twentieth century architectural design contributed to a totally new look. It was plain surfaced and did not accept ornamentation easily. It gave rise to an architecture devoid of ornament.

The materials used in twentieth-century architecture have opened up a number of expressive possibilities, such as cantilevered projections, sloping walls and volumes treated like sculpture. Modern architects are also aware of the effects that can be obtained through materials alone: rough concrete emphasizes the strength of a wall, while glass walls deemphasize it. A wide variety of construction materials are now available and the creative mixing of different materials expands the design options considerably.

The use of materials has been integral with design since the earliest of civilizations. Certain forms are an integral part of the design language for the material. The fusion of materials and form is the absolute aim of all building design. The worst mistakes in design are made by using a material in forms that belong to another material. The close union of material and design seems to be the necessary result of the other, so that it becomes difficult to determine if the design was the result of the material, or if the material was chosen to express the design.

Material:

The substance or substances out of which a thing is or may be constructed.
(from Latin *materia; matter.*)

Adobe
Large, roughly molded, sun-dried clay units of varying sizes.

Mud is one of the oldest and most common raw material for building. It was used either as a solid material on its own, or as infill between timber forms. Mud has no tensile strength so walls had to be massive and thick, and held in place by their own weight. Primitive houses were made of mud and branches, and were built up like a tent around a central tree trunk. Early log huts were constructed of trees, and the spaces between the logs were filled solid with mud.

The use of sun-dried adobe brick was common in all early cultures, particularly in arid lands. (Adobe is a Spanish word from the Arabic *Al-toba*, meaning "the brick.") Early forms of bricks were made of a mixture of mud and straw, molded by hand, and hardened without artificial heat.

The most current use of adobe is associated with the house building of the Pueblo Indians in the Southwestern United States. The forms that they developed are still imitated in the vernacular architecture of that region.

Aluminum
A lightweight metal which is very malleable, nonmagnetic, has good conductivity, a good reflector of heat and light, and resistance to oxidation.

Aluminum is available in sheets and extruded structural shapes. Sheet aluminum is used widely for walls and roofs due to its extreme light weight. Extruded structural shapes are available in a variety of configurations, and are used primarily for grillwork, window sections and door frames. The metal is often "anodized", which provides a hard, nonporous oxide film on the surface, thus protecting it from deteriorating. This coating is available in a wide variety of finishes

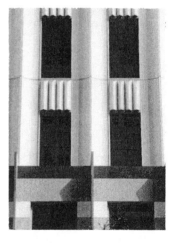

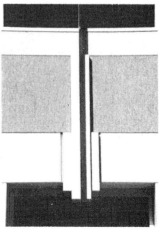

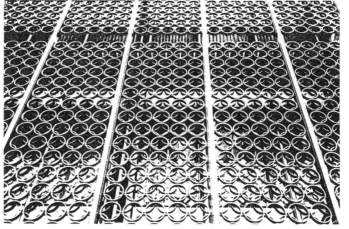

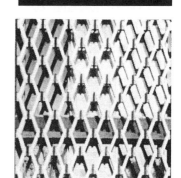

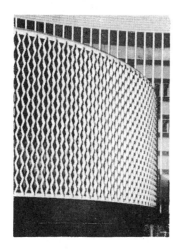

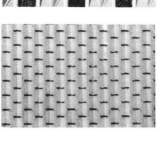

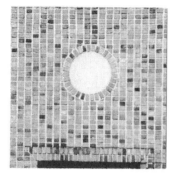

Brick

A solid or hollow masonry unit of clay mixed with sand, and molded into a rectangular shape while in a plastic state, then baked in a kiln.

Bricks are small, uniform building blocks whose size was originally determined by a weight that could be picked up easily with one hand. Traditional brick-making is a very simple process, and bricklaying is a straightforward craft, although ornamental brickwork can be quite complex. Bricks are used for load bearing walls or to face another material such as concrete or concrete block.

The appearance and appeal of brickwork depends on the color, texture, bonding, and the choice of mortar. Bonding is the process of overlapping the courses of bricks, one above the other. The repeating patterns of courses and vertical joints provide the distinguishing characteristic of the brickwork.

There is also a long tradition in the use of ornamentally glazed brickwork. Glazes can be any color, and bricks can be smooth or coarse-grained, with a stippled or combed texture on the surface.

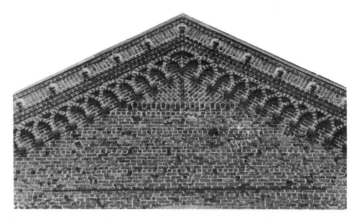

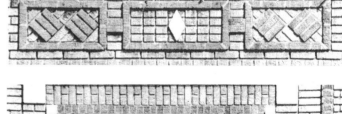

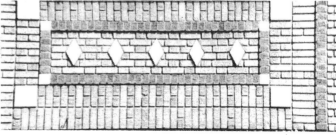

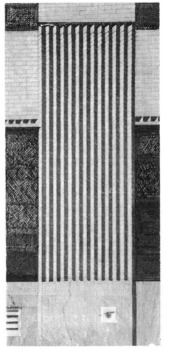

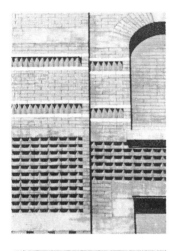

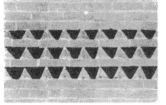

Most brickwork is resolved into a predominant tone and pattern that harmonizes, but contrasts are exploited as well. Some old walls were built with intricate weave patterns. Others used bricks to create shadows by placing them on angles, either at the corners or in panels near window openings.

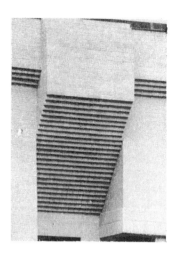

Brick

Bas-relief patterns can be made by cantilevering or recessing bricks, either singly or in groups. All of these techniques can be easily done with ready-made bricks.

Because it is modular, brick offers designers an opportunity to develop decorative systems by working with a few basic shapes that are combined in different ways. Brick has been used to create highly decorative patterns throughout history.

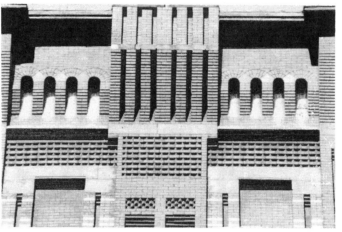

Brick

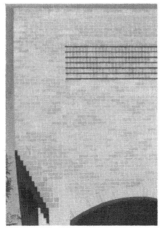

Old bricks vary considerably in color, texture and size, and until recently there remained a great deal of tonal variation between bricks. Today they are manufactured with a more uniform appearance, or with closely controlled, intentional color variations.

The mortar mixture affects the appearance a great deal in terms of thickness, color and pointing methods. Different kinds of pointed joints can create shadows or provide a smooth appearance. Contrasting brickwork has been used since early times. The buildings of the Byzantine period used many decorative brick patterns and bandings, which included diagonals and herringbone bonds. Also checkerboard patterns were very popular as ornamentation in the high Victorian period, and the brickwork was a creative mixture of colors and patterns.

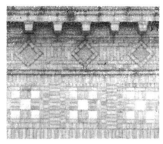

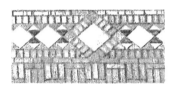

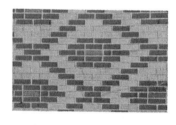

Bricks combine well with other materials. In the Renaissance, brick was combined with stone. In Spain it was alternately blended with stone, and in England it was used in half-timber construction. In Colonial America it was used from the earliest settlements through all the periods and revival styles. In each case brick was mixed with a variety of materials such as stone and wood.

Cast Iron

An iron alloy which is poured into a sand mold and then machined to a desired shape.

Long before it was used as a building material, iron was made into tools and weapons. Cast iron and wrought iron formed decorative ornamental elements. Victorian architecture explored its changeable quality for decoration as well as structurally as frameworks for early skyscrapers. The style also adapted it to steel and glass construction. Art Nouveau periods used it not only for decorative details on their buildings, but for arts and crafts purposes as well.

Ornamental iron is used for grilles, gates, finials, hardware and innumerable architectural accessories. Other ornamental metals, such as bronze, brass, copper, aluminum and stainless steel, are not used for major construction. They have enjoyed a renewal as infill materials. These include copper panels, sheet aluminum, stainless steel, and baked enamel metal alloy panels.

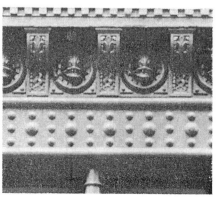

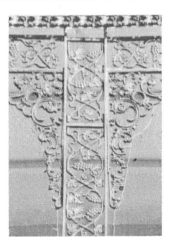

Cast Iron

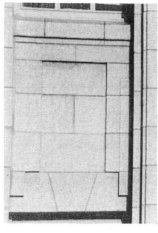

Cast Stone

A mixture of stone chips and Portland cement in a matrix. Once cast it may be ground, polished or otherwise treated to simulate stone.

The properties of cast stone are similar to those of concrete, but due to the added materials it can achieve different finishes. It can look like limestone, brownstone, or sandstone. Its ability to hold fine detail in casting make it appropriate for reproducing both modern and traditional elements and textures. Larger panels are made up of several smaller segments.

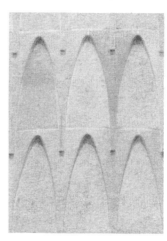

Ceramics

A product made of clay or similar material, fired during manufacture to produce porcelain, or terracotta.

The range of ceramic material in tiles, plaques, and bas-relief ornamentation is unlimited. Texture, color, and shape are virtually without restriction. Size is unlimited also, because large areas can be divided into smaller manageable pieces. The range includes ceramic mosaic tiles, glazed or unglazed, wall tiles made of clay and glazed, and quarry tiles, usually unglazed for use on floors.

Tiles are usually used in groups or bands, such as in horizontal courses; vertically around doors and windows, as moldings; as an overall pattern; or in panels as colored "pictures." They are also found covering dome structures or cupolas.

Concrete

A composite material consisting of an aggregate of broken stone mixed with sand, cement and water. It is fluid and plastic when wet, and hard and strong when dry.

Concrete can be poured into forms and temporary molds when wet, or sprayed on a reinforcing network where it sets up as a strong, durable material. It is little affected by fire and can be exposed to the weather if poured and cured properly.

Exposed concrete is generally unattractive unless it is formed with integral textures. There is another form of concrete which exposes the internal aggregate .Its characteristics depend on the size, color and texture of the panel on which it is formed.

Concrete can also be textured by hammering the surface after it has set. It can be formed with ridges which are later broken off by a hammer. These rough shapes can also be built into the form itself, thus requiring no action once the forms are removed. The texture is already cast in place. Sandblasting is sometimes used to achieve a matte finish.

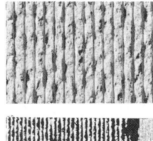

Materials can be inserted into the forms to create special effects, such as wood, plaster and rubber.These inserts can easily be embossed, and the pattern will be transferred to the surface of the concrete in reverse. The most common material used in this manner is wood. The idea is as old as the first arches and vaults, wherein wood members were constructed under the arches to hold them in place during construction. The underside of the arches was covered with a wet plaster, and when the wooden supports were removed the texture of the wood was revealed in the concrete. Special form liners offer the most potential for creating textures and ornamental features, and they are also the least expensive.

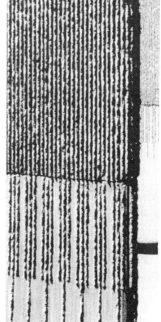

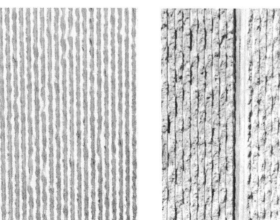

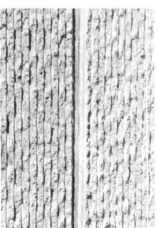

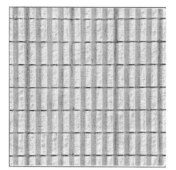

Concrete Block

A hollow but sometimes solid concrete masonry unit, rectangular in shape, made from Portland cement and other aggregates.

A concrets block is much larger than a brick but is manufactured on a modular basis, so that the two materials can be used in the same system of construction. The block is often thought of as a backup material to the brick facing. However, today it is rendered in a wide variety of decorative forms, colors and textures.

These decorative blocks fall into two main categories: well-defined patterns formed in the molding process (vertical ribs), and less precise textures created by breaking the molded block (split face). A split rib surface combines the two techniques. Since these decorative surfaces come in standard modular block sizes, they can be interchanged in a wall to make countless different patterns, from very simple to rich textures and patterns. There is another block which is highly decorative due to its perforations. It allows ventilation while maintaining privacy. It is available in a variety of designs which can be mixed to form different patterns.

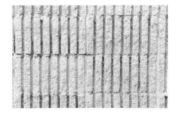
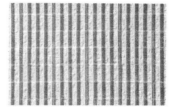
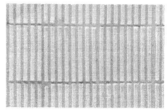

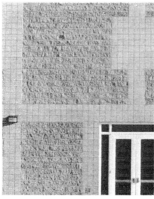

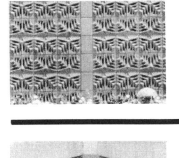

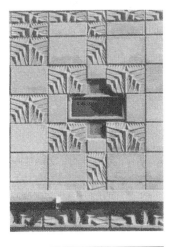

The concrete block was given its highest achievement in the customized designs of Frank Lloyd Wright. He designed many homes using specially made blocks with patterns that were specific only to that residence. They were so unique, even to his own architectural style, that they evolved into a style of their own.

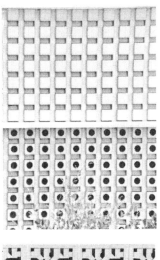

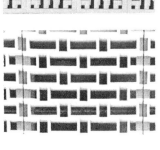

Concrete Grilles
An openwork barrier used to conceal, decorate, or protect an opening.

Concrete blocks have been used for years for foundations and solid walls. An adaptation of the concrete block wall includes a wide variety of grillwork formed by individual blocks with an open pattern cast into each block. The blocks can be arranged in a variety of ways, producing overall textures and patterns. Concrete grillwork provides protection from the sun as well as a degree of privacy, depending on the openness of the grill.

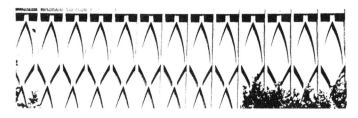

Concrete Panels

Panels that are precast and prefabricated elsewhere and placed in the structure rather than cast in place.

In its natural state, concrete is a material that is extremely strong in compression and very weak in tension. Almost all concrete used in construction today is reinforced by the tensile strength of steel bars, wire mesh, or both. Pouring concrete into a form is not new, but preparing concrete components away from the site is relatively new. Precast concrete reduces the need for on-site formwork.

Other methods of construction using concrete involve a process known as "tilt-up" construction, wherein precast panels are lifted into a vertical position and then attached to the structural frame."Lift-slab" construction involves casting floor and roof slabs one upon another, then jacking or hoisting the slabs into final position. This saves on formwork for cast-in-place floors in a multistory structure.

"Prestressed" concrete is achieved by inserting steel rods into the forms which are anchored to the ends of the forms. These rods are then stretched before pouring, which puts them under tension and deforms them by lengthening them. When the concrete hardens the anchors are released and the rods spring back to their original shape, adding strength to the composite structural member.

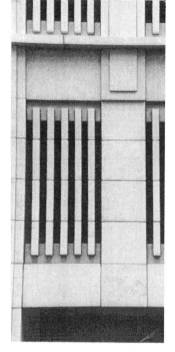

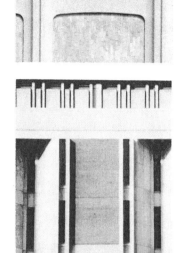

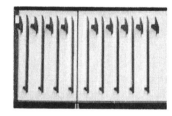

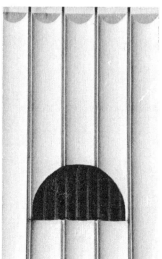

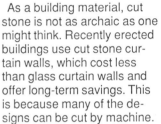

Cut Stone

Any stone cut to a specified size and shape to conform to drawings, for installation in a designated place.

As a building material, cut stone is not as archaic as one might think. Recently erected buildings use cut stone curtain walls, which cost less than glass curtain walls and offer long-term savings. This is because many of the designs can be cut by machine.

Cut stone can be carved by the intaglio method, in which the design is recessed rather than raised above the surface. The most common kinds are granite, limestone, and marble. Granite is the densest of the three. Limestone is composed of the skeletons of billions of sea creatures, deposited on early ocean floors, Marble is stone formed under heat and pressure, and is variegated in color. Vertical slices through the earthshows the concentric layers of different minerals, and this gives the characteristic veining.

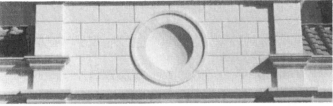

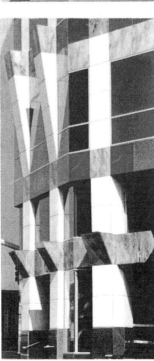

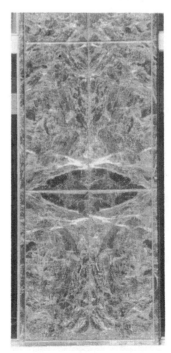

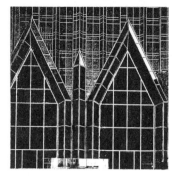

Glass

A hard, brittle transparent or translucent substance, produced by melting a mixture of salica oxides; while molten it may be blown, drawn, rolled, pressed, or cast to a variety of shapes.

Sheet glass was made as early as Roman times, while stained glass originated over two thousand years ago when pieces of colored glass were embedded in heavy matrices of stone or plaster. Leaded glass dates from the Middle Ages, where glass was set into malleable lead frames.

Glass has the properties of allowing clear vision, while offering protection from the elements. Normally it is brittle, but it can also be hardened against breakage by admixtures. It can be made to have more insulating qualities by sandwiching two layers of glass separated by a vacuum sealed edge.

The wide variety of uses includes plate glass for large expanses of distortion-free light, heat-treated tempered glass for additional strength, wire glass for added fire resistance, heat-absorbing glass for reducing solar radiation, insulating glass to reduce heat loss, corrugated glass for decorative interior partitions, and mirror glass for metallic reflecting surfaces. While perfectly plain, glass-sheathed buildings may have no ornamentation, the glass itself provides the decorative effect, as it reflects light and other elements.

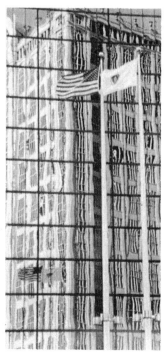

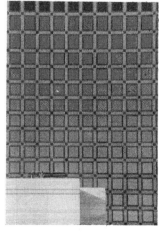

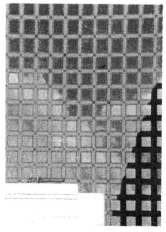

Glass also became a decorative element with embossing and sand-blasting techniques. Beveling created a more subtle form of ornamentation. Etching was another method used to create ornamentation in glass. The Victorian and Art Nouveau styles made widespread use of colored glass in windows and lighting fixtures.

The use of glass in building design has increased immensely in the last decade. Not long ago window glass and mirrors were the only practical applications . Now glass can be transparent, translucent or mirrored; and made nonglare, pigmented, or tinted. It can be shaped by casting, rolling, pressing or baking. It can also be bonded to metal for use as an exterior cladding.

Glass Block
Composed of two sheets of plate glass with an air space between them, formed into a sealed modular hollow block.

They are laid up with mortar, similar to masonry blocks. They are usually transparent, and are made with a wide variety of surface patterns which diffuse the light differently. If stained glass is most often associated with church architecture, glass block is most often associated with modern architecture. Glass block is a modular material, like brick, and comes in several distinct styles, patterns and degrees of transparency and translucency.

Masonry

Includes all stone products, all brick products and all concrete block units, including decorative and customized blocks.

Ashlar masonry consists of smooth square stones laid with mortar in horizontal courses. A contrasting type of masonry is rubble, which consists of very irregular stones. It is used primarily in the construction of foundations and walls where the irregular quality is desirable.

Rusticated masonry is another coursed stone, in which each block is separated by deep joints. The surface is usually very rough. Quarry-faced stone is composed of squared blocks, with rough surfaces that look as if they just came out of the ground.

Cyclopean masonry is often found in some ancient cultures, and is characterized by huge irregular stones that are laid without mortar and without any form of coursing.

To round out the types of masonry, brick and dressed stone were used for door and window surrounds, where regularly shaped blocks are a necessity. These were also laid in horizontal courses, making a decorative contrast banding the walls.

Metals

All metals are mined in a form called "ore" and are manufactured to specific applications.

Most natural metals must be protected from deterioration when exposed to the elements. Each metal has different properties and specific applications.

Iron is hard and brittle and must be cast into shape. Steel is hard and malleable when heated, and is used for structural shapes due to its high tensile strength. Aluminum is lightweight and used in minor structural framing, curtain walls, window frames, doors, flashing and many types of hardware. Copper alloys are extremely good electrical conductors, but are most commonly used for roofing, flashing, hardware and plumbing applications. When exposed to the air, copper oxidizes and develops a greenish "patina" that halts further corrosion. Brass and bronze are alloys that are superior in workability and are used in castings for finish hardware.

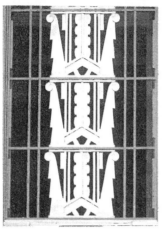

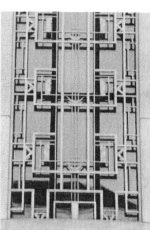

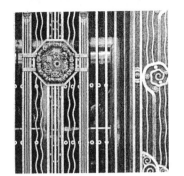

RAYMOND COMMERCE BUILDING

Mosaic

A process of inlaying small pieces of stone, tile, glass or enamel into a cement or plaster matrix.

The art of mosaics is an ancient one. It is an art of assemblage, wherein individual pieces are formed into a total picture or surface. The inside forms of domes and pendentive shapes of early Christian and Byzantine churches were covered with rich mosaics, consisting mostly of small colored tiles, often gilded.

Less traditional uses include the tile-covered sinuous forms of Antonio Gaudi, who used pieces of broken tile and glass set into cement forms. These appear on rooftops of apartment houses and in the public park of Barcelona.

A counterpart of this technique can be found in the Watts Towers of Los Angeles, built by an Italian immigrant, Simon Rodia, over a period of thirty years. Materials include broken pieces of bottle glass, mirrors, shells and shattered dishes, all on a framework of wire mesh and concrete. Specific elements can be identified from close up, but from a distance a richness in color and pattern is produced.

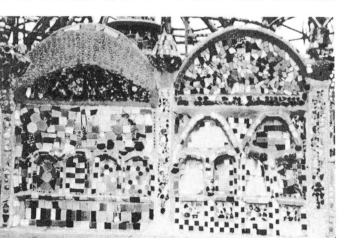

Plaster and Stucco

A mixture of lime or gypsum, sand, Portland cement and water produces a paste-like material which later sets to form a hard surface.

It has always been customary to hide some raw materials of construction behind protective coats of plaster or cement. This practice goes back to the earliest buildings of Egypt. In fact, all the tools of the plasterer were depicted on the walls of the tombs and pyramids. Even in Greece, powdered marble dust made a protective coating that also became a ground for brightly painted surfaces.

Plaster surfaces can be rough or smooth, decorated, or even finished in imitation of another material. It can be molded into ornamental motifs. It is a paradox that our ancestors used plaster to refine the surface of their rough materials, and we now roughen and texture the surfaces of our synthetic materials to replicate the handiwork of earlier times.

Plaster was also used to cover entire walls since it could withstand the settling and movement of the material beneath it. When patterns were inscribed into the wet plaster, it then became a decorative feature which is now called pargeting.

Plastics

Any of the various complex organic compounds produced by polymerization. They can be molded, extruded, or cast into various shapes or drawn into filaments and used as fibers.

For decades designers have been using plastics on the interior of buildings. On the exteriors it is found only in the form of signs and molded panels. Manufacturers are beginning to offer finely detailed moldings, pediments, corners and other elements in light-weight polymers. These can be worked with standard tools and can withstand weathering very well. These materials can be used to replace traditional styles in renovations.

The development of vinyls and other laminates provided flexibility in designing with permanent, wear-resistant, easily maintained material. There are several commercial nicknames for this synthetic material that has the property of being easily shaped and molded. One of the most well-known is "plexiglass," used for windows and lighting fixtures. Others include insulating materials; "fiberglass," "styrofoam," and "urethane." For adhesives and caulkings there are "epoxys," and "silicons" for water- repellant use.

The use of plastics in the entire building industry has increased in recent years from its initial use as insulation to membranes for air-supported structures. Many tensile forms are created by the use of a plastic, or plasticized fabric. Many of these structures are for temporary use, or for seasonal use, but the material can also be permanent.

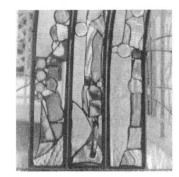

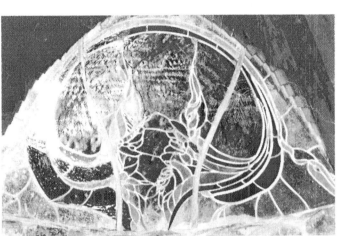

Stained Glass

Glass is given its desired color while in a molten state, or by firing a stain into the surface of the glass after forming. It is used in decorative windows set in lead cames, or cast into a concrete mold as a transparent mosaic.

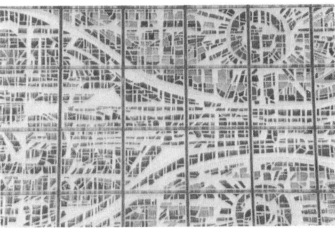

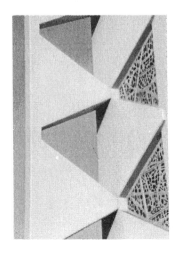

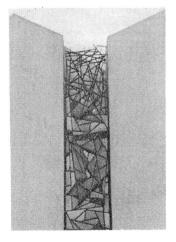

Steel

A malleable alloy of iron and carbon produced by melting and refining according to the carbon content.

Classically steel has been used for the structural framework of large buildings, but it was always hidden from view in the final design. Now steel is used for its aesthetic qualities, as exposed frames and other members.

The aesthetic exploration of steel led modern architects to derive a new style from structural steel members in high-rise office and apartment towers. In fact the steel skeleton has to be encased in a fireproof material, and the steel is therefore largely decorative. Its only function is to support the curtain wall skin.

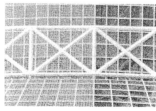

Steel

Steel

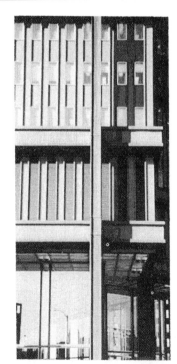

Stone

*Native rock that has been proc-
essed by shaping, cutting or
sizing for building or land-scap-
ing use.*

This is a relatively heavy
material and requires more
skill to work than timber or
brick. It is fire-resistant and
varies according to type, from
fairly porous to impregnable.

There are three basic types
of stone; igneous such as
granite, is long lasting and
durable; sedimentary, such as
limestone is made up of organic remains. Metamorphic
rock is either igneous or sedimentary transformed by pressure and heat or both. Marble
is typical of this type.

The character of stone affects its potential for building
and ornamental use. Hard
stone led to severe and plain
styles, while softer ones in-
vited carved sculpture and
rich embellishment.

Only recently is stone a luxury, with the cost of quarrying
and stone masons pricing it
out of consideration. Stone is
now used as veneers, and
there aremany materials that
imitate stone. Concrete has
all but replaced stone entirely,
although it is used as facings
on high-rise buildings, and as
a veneer on a lot of steel
frame construction.

Terracotta

Fired clay producing a hard unglazed surface, used for ornamental work or roof and floor tile.

This is an ancient material; the term comes from Latin meaning "cooked earth." It is essentially the same material as brick, but is harder since it is baked in a mold. It may be either its natural brown color, or glazed. It was used since early times as an integral decorative material for wall surfaces, or roof or floor tiles.

Terracotta ornament can be classified into five types: supports (columns and pilasters); bands (friezes and cornices); panels (overall patterns); and free ornaments (rosettes and finials). Each type occurred at specific places: the supports at the building base, cap and corner; bands between major horizontal divisions; panels between windows; free ornaments as accents at the roof line corners and the intersections of major elements. Wall surfaces between the glazed terracotta elements were generally of brick.

Tile

Any of a class of product made of clay or similar material that is subjected to a high temperature and has either a glazed or nonglazed surface. They are manufactured in many configurations.

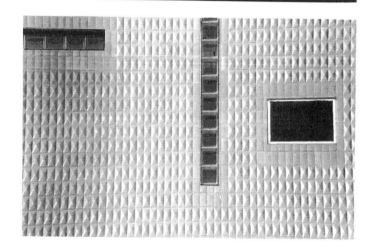

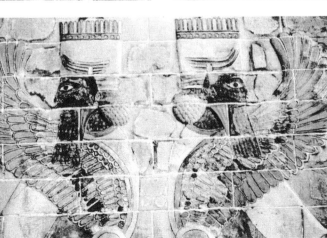

Tile

Ceramic mosaic tile
An unglazed tile, usually mounted on sheets to facilitate setting, may be either composed of porcelain or natural clay.

Clay tile
A roofing tile of hard, burnt clay. In flooring it is called a quarry tile.

Crest tile
Tile which fits like a saddle on the ridge of a roof.

Encaustic tile
A tile for pavement and wall decoration, in which the pattern is inlaid or incrusted in clay of one color in a ground of clay of another color .

Glazed tile
Ceramic tile having a fused impervious glazed surface finish, composed of ceramic materials fused into the body of the tile; the body may be nonvitreous, semivitreous, or impervious.

Mission tile
A clay roofing tile, approximately semicylindrical in shape; laid in courses with the units having their convex side alternating up and down.

Paving tile
Unglazed porcelain or natural clay tile, formed by the dust-pressed method; similar to ceramic mosaic tile in composition and physical properties, but thicker.

Ridge tile
A tile which is curved in section, often decorative, used to cover the ridge of a roof.

Unglazed tile
A hard, dense ceramic tile for floor or walls; of homogeneous composition, and deriving its color and texture from the materials and the method of manufacture.

Tile

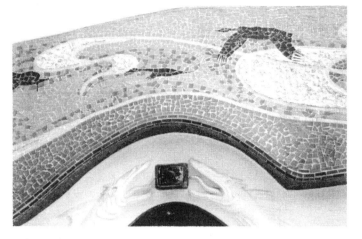

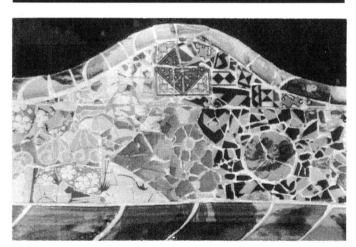

Timber/ Wood Products

Uncut trees suitable for construction are converted to lumber or lumber products by sawing, planing,or rotary cutting to produce standardized sizes of rough or dressed lumber.

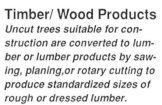

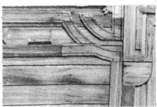

Wood has been used for house design since the most primitive dwelling, particularly in forested areas. It was the staple building material. Most primitive structures employed wood branches covered with mud or straw. Other early forms of wood dwellings were log huts which developed into what are called long houses due to their elongated shape, most likely for communal living.

In more recent times wood cladding dates from the eighteenth century, and was traditionally used as overlapping planks. Wood was also used ornamentally throughout Medieval European architecture, as carved beams, door and window frames, and carved barge-boards.

It was customary to cover timber frames with horizontal boards. Originally, they were tapered and overlapped each other; the rough bark edge was kept on the bottom side. Gradually the boards were milled smoother and more uniform, and eventually the siding was beveled so that it could be overlapped more easily.

Timber / Wood Products

Timber / Wood Products

The Victorian craze for decorative woodwork was due in part to the invention of the jigsaw and the lathe for producing turned wooden ornamental elements.

The development of new structural wood forms using plywood and other laminates has revolutionized the structural use of wood. New bonding techniques have opened new applications for plywood.

Stressed skin panels are constructed of plywood and seasoned lumber. The simple framing and plywood skin act as a total unit to resist loads.

Glue-laminated arches and beams now span extremely long distances. "Glu-lams" are fabricated from layers of wood that are joined together with adhesives.

Box beams consist of one or more vertical plywood webs laminated to seasoned wood flanges. Vertical spacers separate the flanges at intervals along the length of the beam to distribute the loads and to provide stiffness.

Folded plate roofs are thin skins of plywood reinforced by purlins to form structures of great strength. Use of folded plates eliminates the need for truss systems.

Wrought Iron
An easily forged iron containing carbon. It can be hammered into shapes, either when hot or cold, and is used as decorative grilles for window openings, entryways, or balcony railings.

Many terms have been used to describe those parts of our surroundings that have been conceived and built in previous eras. There are literally layer upon layer of creative experience to draw upon. To fully appreciate this built environment we need to know a little about its language. To many people, things like mullions, lintels, buttress and fenestration are terms only historians use. A familiarity with the basic terminology regarding components of the built environment provides a common language with which to understand and share concepts about structures, both old and new. When the visual images and reactions are broken down into verbal terms, a vocabulary of components enables us to communicate concerns about the built environment including the importance of preserving it.

The elements that make up a building can refer to specific things and physical items such as doors, windows, walls and roofs, as well as to abstract items such as form, line, color, texture and other elements of design and composition. These abstract items are covered in the chapter on composition. Components include all the items found in the major masses, openings, voids, bases and capitals, and a wide variety of detail both functional and ornamental.

While most glossaries of building components are word descriptions only, with small illustrations in the sidebars, this one is just the opposite. Each component is illustrated with a photograph, series of photographs, or pages of photographs. This features the component in many different situations from many styles, different materials and numerous design solutions. While it would be possible to totally isolate each component, none exists in a vacuum, and so they are presented as an integrated part of the structure exactly as they were originally built. Many of the case studies show old and new side by side.

Components:

A simple part, or a relatively complex entity regarded as a part of a system; element; constituent. (from Latin componens; to place together.)

Abacus

The flat area at the top of a capital, dividing a column from its entablature. It usually consists of a square block, or enriched with moldings. In some orders the sides are hollowed and the angles at the corner are truncated.

Abutment

A masonry mass, pier, or solid part of a wall that takes the lateral thrust of an arch.

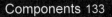

Acanthus

A common plant of the Mediterranean, whose leaves, stylized, form the characteristic decoration of capitals of the Corinthian and Composite orders. In scroll form it appears on friezes and panels.

Accolade

A rich ornamental treatment made up of two ogee curves meeting in the middle, as over a door, window, or arch.

Acropodium

An elevated pedestal bearing a statue that is raised above the substructure.

Acroteria

A pedestal for statues and other ornaments placed on the apex and the lower angles of a pediment; or often refers to the ornament itself.

Addorsed

Animals or figures that are placed back to back and featured as decorative sculpture over doors, in pediments, medallions, and other ornamental devices.

Affronted

Figures or animals that are placed facing each other, as decorative features over doors and in pediments.

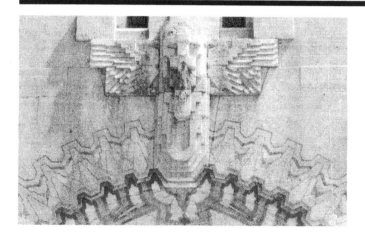

Agraffe

The keystone section of an arch, especially when carved with a cartouche or human face.

Anchor

A metal device fastened on the outside of a wall and tied to the end of a rod or metal strap connecting it with an opposite wall, to prevent bulging; often consisting of a fanciful decorative design.

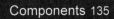

Angle column
A free-standing or engaged
column placed at the corner of
a building or portico.

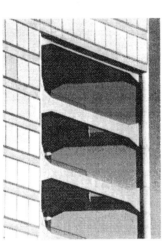

Anta

A pier or pilaster formed by a thickening at the end of a wall, most often used on the side of a doorway or beyond the face of an end wall.

Anthemion

A common Greek ornament based on the honeysuckle or palmette, used in a radiating cluster, either singly on a stele or antefix, or as a running ornament on friezes.

Antic

A grotesque sculpture consisting of animals, human and foliage forms incongruously run together and used to decorate molding terminations and other parts of medieval architecture.

Apex
The highest point, peak, or tip
of any structure.

Apex

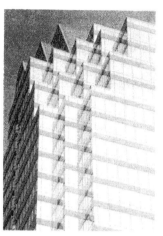

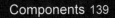

Apex

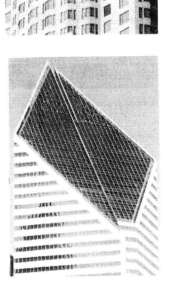

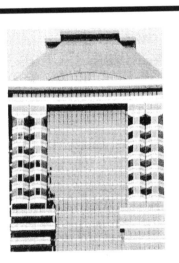

Apex stone
The uppermost stone in a gable, pediment, vault, or dome, usually triangular, often highly decorated.

Applied trim
Supplementary and separate decorative strips of wood or moldings applied to the face or sides of a frame.

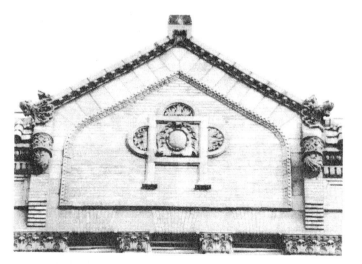

Applique
An accessory decorative feature applied to a structure. In ornamental work, one material affixed to another.

Arabesque
Generic term for an intricate
and subtle ornate surface
decoration based on a mixture
of intermixed geometrical
patterns and natural botanical
forms used in Muhammadan
countries.

Arbor
A light open latticework frame,
often used as a shady garden
shelter or bower.

Arcade

A line of arches along one or both sides, supported by pillars or columns, either as free-standing or attached to a building. Applies to a line of arches fronting shops, and covered with a steel and glass skylight, usually running the length of the arcade.

Arcade

Arch

A basic architectural structure built over an opening, made up of wedge-shaped blocks, keeping one another in position, and transferring the vertical pressure of the superimposed load into components transmitted laterally to the adjoining abutments.

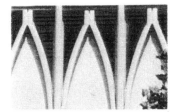

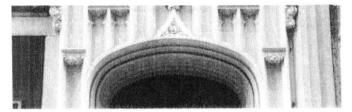

Acute arch
A sharply pointed two-centered arch whose centers of curvature are farther apart than the opening.

Basket handle arch
A flattened arch designed by joining a quarter circle to each end of a false ellipse; a three-centered arch with a crown whose radius is greater than the outer pair of curves.

Bell arch
A round arch resting on two large corbels with curved faces.

Blind arch
An arch within a wall that contains a recessed flat wall rather than framing an opening. Used to enrich an otherwise unrelieved expanse of masonry.

Blunt arch
An arch rising only to a slight point struck from two-centers within the arch.

Broken arch
A form of segmental arch in which the center of the arch is omitted and is replaced by a decorative feature usually applied to a wall above the entablature over a door or window.

Camber arch

A flat segmental arch with a slightly upward curve in the intrados and sometimes also in the extrados.

Cinquefoil arch

A five-lobed pattern divided by cusps; a cusped arch with five foliations worked into the intrados; a cinquefoil tracery at the apex of a window.

Circular arch

An arch whose intrados takes the form of a segment of a circle.

Compound arch

An arch formed by concentric arches set within one another

Corbel arch

A false arch constructed by corbeling courses from each side of an opening until they meet at a mid-point; a capstone is laid on top to complete it.

Crescent arch

A type of horseshoe arch.

Cusped arch
An arch which has cusps or foliations worked into the intrados.

Diminished arch
An arch having less rise or height than a semicircle.

Discharging arch
An arch, usually segmental and often a blind arch, built above the lintel of a door or window to discharge the weight of the wall above the lintel to each side.

Extradosed arch
An arch in which the extrados is clearly marked, as a curve exactly or roughly nearly parallel to the intrados; it has a well-marked archivolt.

False arch
A form having the appearance of an arch, though not of arch construction, such as a corbeled arch.

Flat arch
An arch with a horizontal, or nearly horizontal intrados, with little or no convexity; an arch with a horizontal intrados with voussoirs radiating from a center below.

Florentine arch

An arch whose entrados is not concentric with the intrados, and whose voussoirs are therefore longer at the crown than at the springing, common in Florence in the early Renaissance.

Gauged arch
An arch of wedge-shaped bricks which have been shaped so that the jambs radiate from a common center.

Horseshoe arch
A rounded arch whose curve is wider than a semi-circle, so that the opening at the bottom is narrower than its greatest span.

Inverted arch
An arch with its intrados below the springline, especially used to distribute concentrated loads in foundations.

lancet arch
Same as an acute arch.

Mayan arch
A corbeled arch of triangular shape common in the buildings of the Maya Indians of Yucatan.

Obtuse-angle arch
A type of pointed arch, formed by arcs of circles that intersect at the apex; the center of the circles are nearer together than the width of the arch.

Ogee arch
A pointed arch composed of reversed curves, the lower concave, the upper convex; a pointed arch, each haunch of which Is a double curve with the concave side uppermost.

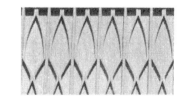

Pointed arch
Any arch with a point at its apex, characteristic of but not limited to Gothic architecture.

Rampant arch
An arch in which the impost on one side is higher than that on the other.

Rear arch
An inner arch of an opening which is smaller in size than the exterior arch of the opening and which may be a different shape.

Recessed arch
An arch with a shorter radius set within another of the same shape.

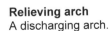

Relieving arch
A discharging arch.

Roman arch
A semicircular arch in which all units are wedge-shaped.

Round arch
An arch having a continuously curved intrados, often semi-circular.

Rowlock arch
An arch wherein the bricks or small voussoirs are arranged in separate concentric rings.

Semi-arch
An arch in which only one half of its sweep is developed, as in a flying buttress.

Stepped arch
An arch in which the outer ends of some or all of the voussoirs are cut square to fit Into the horizontal courses of the wall at the sides of the arch.

Stilted arch
An arch whose curve begins above the impost line; one resting on imposts treated as a downward continuation of the archivolt.

Surbased arch
An arch having a rise of less than half the span.

Trefoil arch
An arch having a cusped in-trados with three round or pointed foils.

Triangular arch
A structure composed of two stones laid diagonally, mutu-ally supporting each other to span an opening; a primitive form of arch consisting of two stones laid diagonally to sup-port each other over an opening.

Architrave
The lowest of the three divisions of a classical entablature, the main beam spanning from column to column, resting directly on the capitals.

Archivolt
The ornamental molding running around the exterior curve of an arch, around the openings of windows, doors, and other openings.

Archivolt

Arena
A space of any shape surrounded by seats rising in tiers surrounding a stage; a type of theater without a proscenium.

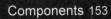

Atlas
A figure of a man used in place of a column to support an entablature; also called Atlantes and Telemon.

Atrium
The forecourt of an early Christian basilica, with colonnades on all four sides, and usually a fountain in the center. It was derived from the entrance court or hall of a Roman dwelling, roofed to leave a large opening to admit light. Rain was received in a cistern below. The modern version is a common space with skylights in an office or hotel complex.

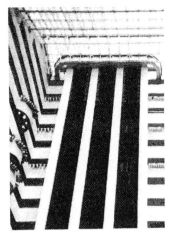

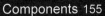

Atrium

Auditorium
That part of a theater, school, or public building that is set aside for the listening and viewing audience.

Awning
A roof-like cover of canvas or other lightweight material, extending in front of a door-way or window, or over a deck, providing protection from the sun or rain.

Balcony

A projecting platform usually on the exterior of a building, sometimes supported from below by brackets or corbels, or cantilevered by projecting members of wood, metal or masonry. They are most often enclosed with a railing, balustrade, or other parapet. Balconies provide an extension for the interior rooms, and are most often designed as an integral part of the structure, and related to the style of the building. It can be enclosed with solid railings or grillwork, onamented with wrought ironwork are left un-adorned.

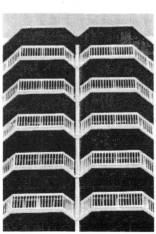

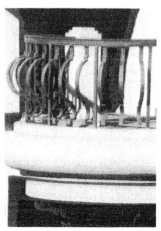

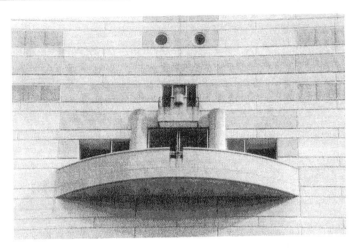

Baluster
One of a number of short vertical members used to support a stair railing.

Baluster column
A short, thick-set column in a subordinate position, as in the windows of early Italian Renaissance facades.

Balustrade
An entire railing system, as along the edge of a balcony, including a top rail, bottom rail and balusters.

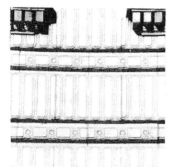

Band

A flat horizontal fascia, or a continuous member or series of moldings projecting slightly from the wall plane, encircling a building or along a wall, that makes a division in the wall.

Banded rustication

Alternating smooth ashlar and roughly textured stone.

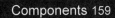

Banding
Horizontal subdivisions of a column or wall using profile or material change.

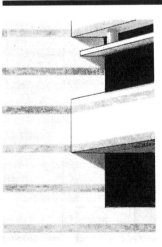

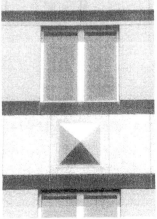

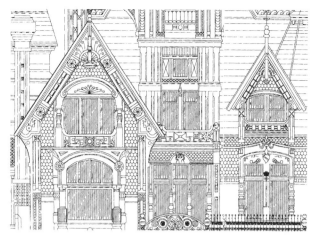

Bargeboard

A trim board used on the edge of gables where the roof extends over the wall; it either covers the rafter or occupies the place of a rafter. Originally it was ornately carved.

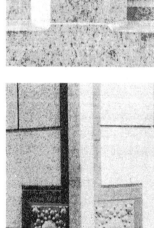

Base

The lowest part of a pillar. wall, or building. The base, or plinth, commonly takes the same form as the moldings. In some styles where there are clustered pillars in which there are small shafts of different sizes. the bases become more complex as they modulate between the floor and the wall or column group above them.

Batten

A narrow strip of wood that is applied over a joint between parallel boards in the same plane. In roofing, a strip applied over boards or structural members as a base for attaching slate , wood, or clay shingles.

Battlement

A parapet having a regular alternation of solid parts and openings, originally for defense, but later used as a decorative motif.

Bay
A principal compartment or division in the architectural arrangement of a building. marked either by buttresses or pilasters in the wall, by the disposition of the main arches and pillars, or by any repeated spatial units that separate it into corresponding portions.

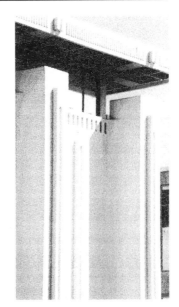

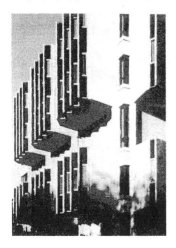

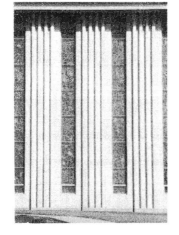

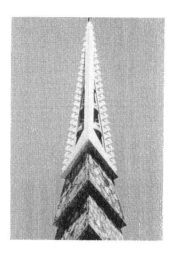

Belfry
A room at or near the top of a tower that contains bells and their supporting timbers.

Bell turret
A small tower, usually topped with a spire or pinnacle, containing one or more bells.

Belvedere
A building, architectural feature, or rooftop pavilion from which a vista can be enjoyed.

Bent
A framework, which is transverse to the length of a framed structure; usually designed to carry both a lateral and a vertical load.

Beton Brut
Concrete textured by leaving the impression of the form in which it was molded. as in when wood is used to create a grained surface effect.

Bezant
An ornament shaped like a coin or disc. sometimes used in a series in decorative molding designs.

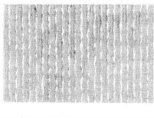

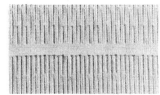

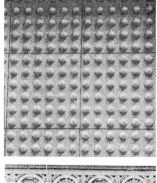

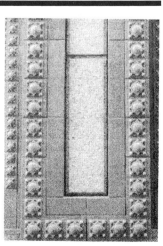

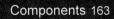

Bond

A system of overlapping rows or courses of stones or bricks used to provide stability and strength in the construction of walls. There are a large number of standard designs and patterns.

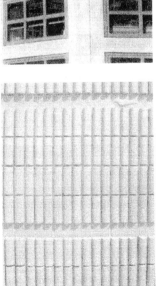

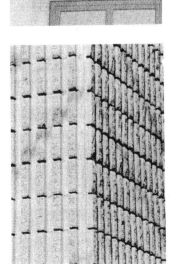

Basketweave bond
A checkerboard pattern of bricks, laid either horizontally and vertically, or laid on the diagonal.

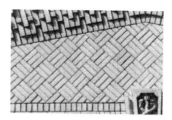

Common bond
A bond in which every fifth or sixth course consists of headers, the other courses by stretchers.

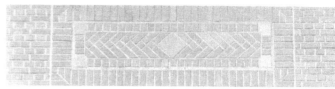

Diagonal bond
A type of raking bond in masonry walls, consisting of a header course with the bricks laid at a diagonal in the face of the wall.

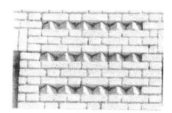

Dogtooth course
A stringcourse of bricks laid diagonally so that one corner projects beyond the face of the wall.

Flemish bond

In brickwork, a bond in which each course consists of headers and stretchers laid alternately, each header is centered with respect to the stretcher above and the stretcher below it.

Flemish diagonal bond
A bond in which a course of alternate headers and stretchers is followed by a course of stretchers, resulting in a diagonal pattern.

Rowlock
A brick laid on its edge so that its end is exposed; used on a sloping window sill, or to cap a low brick wall.

Stack bond
In brickwork, a patterned bond where the facing brick is laid with all vertical joints aligned; in stone veneer masonry, a pattern in which single units are set with continuous vertical and horizontal joints.

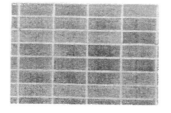

Border

A margin, rim, or edge around or along an element; a design or a decorative strip on the edge of an element.

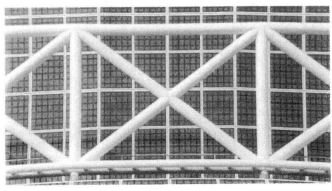

Cross bracing

A pair of diagonal braces crossing each other to stabilize a structural frame against lateral forces.

Diagonal bracing

A system of inclined members for bracing the angles between the members of a structural frame against horizontal forces, such as wind.

Lateral bracing

Stabilizing a wall beam or structural system against lateral forces by means of diagonal or cross bracing, either horizontally by roof or floor construction or vertically by pilasters, columns or cross walls.

Bracket
A projection from a vertical surface providing structural or visual support under cornices. balconies. Windows, or any other overhanging member.

Bracket

Bridge

A structure which spans a depression or provides a passage between two points at a height above the ground affording passage for pedestrians and vehicles. A footbridge is a narrow structure designed to carry pedestrians only. A skywalk is located over the ground level and the street. and often connects buildings across a street.

Bridge

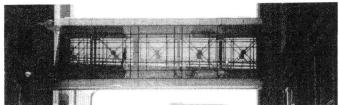

Bridge

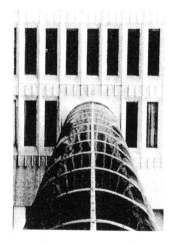

Bridge

Building artifact
An element on a building demonstrating human crafting, such as a stained-glass window or an ornament of archaeological or historic interest .

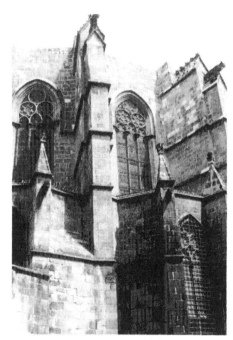

Buttress
An exterior mass of masonry projecting from the wall to create additional strength and support, absorbing the lateral thrusts from roof vaults. They often stand out boldly and are either unbroken in their height or broken into stages, with a successive reduction in their projection and in their width. The set-offs dividing these stages are generally sloped at a very acute angle. They terminate at the top with a plain slope dying into the wall or with a triangular pediment.

Campanile
A bell tower detached from the main body of a church.

Canephora
An ornament representing a young maiden bearing a basket of ceremonial offerings on her head, used either as a column support or as a free-standing garden ornament.

Canopy
A decorative hood above a niche, pulpit, or stall; a covered area that extends from the wall of a building, protecting an enclosure.

Cantilever
A structural member or any other element projecting beyond its supporting wall or column and weighted at one end to carry a proportionate weight on the projecting end.

Capital

The upper member of a column, pillar, pier or pilaster. It is usually decorated. It may carry an architrave, arcade or impost block. In classical architecture the orders each have their respective capitals, which differ significantly from one another. In later periods they are endlessly diversified.

Angle capital
A capital occurring at a corner column, especially an Ionic capital where the four volutes project equally on the diagonals, instead of along two parallel planes.

Basket capital
A capital with interlaced bands resembling the weave of a basket, found in Byzantine architecture.

Blfron capital
A capital with two fronts or faces looking in two directions, similar to a double herm.

Campaniform capital
A bell shaped Egyptian capital representing an open papyrus profile.

Composite capital
One of the five classical orders which combines acanthus leaves of the Corinthian order with the volutes of the Ionic order.

Cushlon capital
A capital resembling a cushion that is weighted down; in medieval architecture, a cubic capital with its lower angles rounded off.

Geminated capital
Coupled or dual capitals.

Lotus capital
In ancient Egyptian architecture, a capital having the shape of a lotus bud.

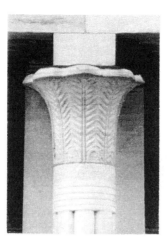

Palm capital
A type of Egyptian capital resembling the spreading crown of a palm tree; a column capital resembling the leaves of a palm tree.

Papyriform capital
A capital of an Egyptian column with the form of a cluster of papyrus flowers.

Quadrafron capital
Having four fronts or faces looking in four directions.

Scalloped capital
A medieval block or cushion capital, when each lunette is developed into several truncated cones.

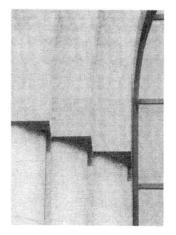

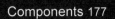

Cartouche
A decorative ornamental tablet resembling a scroll of paper with the center either inscribed or left plain, but framed with an elaborate scroll-like carving.

Carved work
In stonework, any hand-cut ornamental features that cannot be applied from patterns.

Caryatid
A supporting member serving the function of a pier, column, or pilaster, and carved and molded in the form of a draped human figure; in Greek architecture, as in the Erectheum at the Acropolis in Athens.

Caryatid

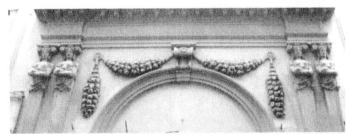

Casing
A trim member, molding, framing or lining around, door and window openings which give a finished appearance. They may be flat or molded.

Castellated
Bearing the external fortification elements of a castle, in particular, battlements, turrets, crenellated patterns.

Castellation
A notched or indented parapet, originally used for fortifications, but afterwards used on church facades and was intended as ornament.

Cast-iron facade
A load-bearing facade composed of prefabricated parts, commonly used on buildings around 1850-1870.

Castle
A stronghold, building, or group of buildings intended primarily to serve as a fortified post; a fortified residence of a nobleman.

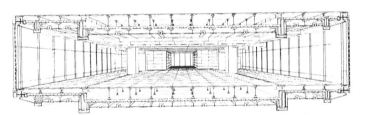

Ceiling
The undercovering of a roof, or floor, generally concealing the structural members from the room or roof above, or the underside surface of vaulting. It may have a flat or curved surface, and may be self-supporting, suspended from the floor above, or supported from hidden or exposed beams.

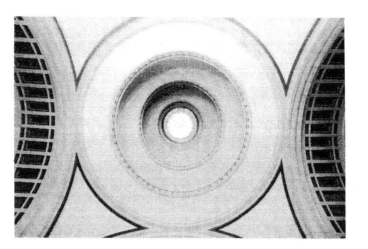

Ceiling

Cella

The sanctuary of a classical temple containing the cult statue of the god.

Centerpiece

An ornament placed in the middle of an area, such as a decoration in the center of a ceiling.

Chamfer

The groove or oblique surface made when an edge or corner is beveled or cut away, usually at a 45 degree angle.

Chamfered rustication

Rustication in which the smooth face of the stone parallel to the wall is deeply beveled at the joints so that, when the two meet, the chamfering forms an internal right angle.

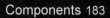

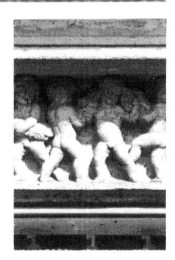

Cherubs

In Renaissance architecture and derivatives, decorative sculpture representing chubby, usually naked infants; also called putti or amorini.

Chimney
A noncombustible structure containing one or more flues, serving a fireplace.

Cincture
A ring of moldings around the top or bottom of the shaft of a column, separating the shaft from the capital or base; a fillet around a post.

Clerestory
An upper story or row of windows rising above the adjoining parts of the building, designed as a means of admitting increased light into the inner space of the building,

Clock
Any instrument for measuring or indicating time, especially a mechanical device with a numbered dial and moving hands or pointers.

Clock

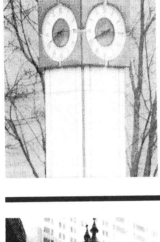

Clock

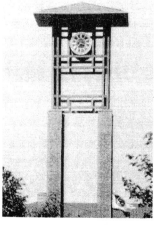

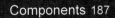

Clocktower
Any instrument for measuring or indicating time, such as a mechanical device with a numbered dial and moving hands or pointers positioned in a single tower, or a tower-like portion of a structure.

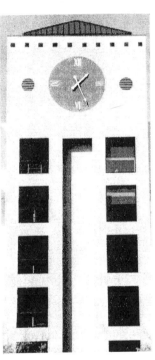

Cloister
A square court surrounded by an open arcade, a covered walk around a courtyard, or the whole courtyard.

Coffer
A recessed box-like panel in a ceiling or vault, usually square, but often octagonal or lozenge shaped, sometimes dressed with simple moldings or elaborately ornamented.

Colonette
A small column, usually decorative, found at the edge of windows; a thin round shaft to give a vertical line in elevation, or as an element in a compound pier.

Colonnade
A combination or grouping of columns paced at regular intervals, and arranged with regard to their structural or ornamental relationship to the building. They can be aligned either straight or arced in a circular pattern.

Column
Centuries of building have created an inexhaustable variety of forms for columns. The proportioning and decoration of a column serves as an indication and characterization of a particular architectural style. A column has a relationship with the ground at the base, and the load it carries from above as expressed in the design of the capital.

Column

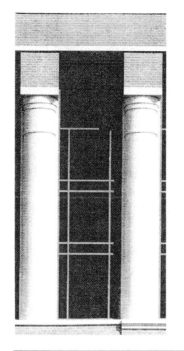

Angle column
A free-standing or engaged column placed outside a corner of a building or portico.

Banded column
A column or pilaster with drums alternately larger and smaller, alternately plainer and richer in decoration, or alternately protruding.

Clustered column
A column or pillar composed of a cluster of attached or semi-attached additional shafts, grouped together to act as a single structural or design element.

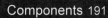

Clustered columns

Coupled column
Columns set as close pairs with a much wider space between the pairs.

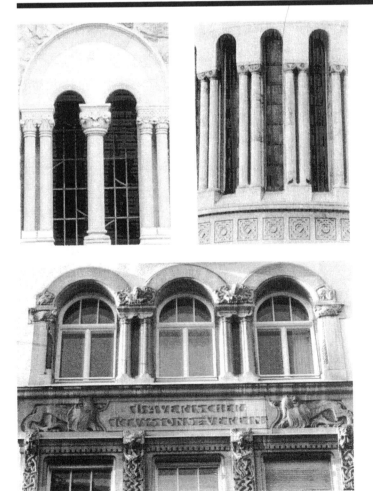

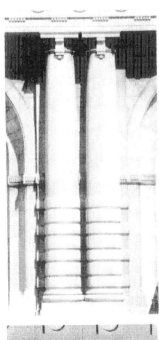

Coupled columns

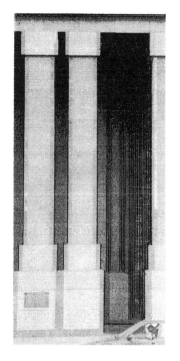

Diminished column
A column with a greater diameter at its base than at its capital.

Engaged column
A column that is attached and appears to emerge from the wall, as decoration or as a structural buttress.

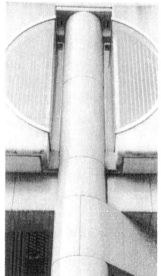

Grouped columns
Three or more closely spaced columns or pilasters forming a group, often on one pedestal.

Half-column
An engaged column projecting approximately one half its diameter, usually slightly more.

Insulated column
A column which is entirely detached from a main building or structure.

Wall column
A column which is embedded or partially embedded in a wall.

Wreathed column
A column entwined by a band that presents a twisted or spiral appearance; a twisted column.

Column Baseplate
A horizontal plate beneath the bottom of a column which transmits and distributes the column load to the supporting materials below the plate.

Conservatory
A glass enclosed room in a house, originally for the cultivation of plants, now including solariums and greenhouses.

Console
A vertical decorative bracket in the form of a scroll, projecting from a wall to support a cornice, window, or a piece of sculpture.

Corbel
In masonry construction, a row of brick projected further outward as it rises to support a cornice.

Corbel Table
A projecting course of masonry supported on corbels near the top of a wall, as a parapet or cornice.

Corbiestep
The stepped edge of an incline that terminates a masonry gable end-wall, masking the surface of a pitched roof beyond; found in northern European masonry construction.

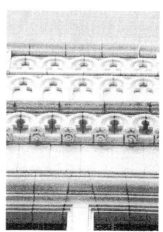

Corner

The position at which two lines or surfaces meet; the immediate exterior of the angle formed by the two lines or surfaces, as in the corner of a building or structure. The corner is one of the most important zones expressing the junction of two facades. Corners can take many forms such as, recessed, rounded, retracted. framed or stepped in shape. They can be angular, curved, or articulated in many different ways.

Corner

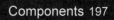

Corner

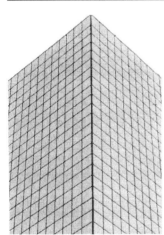

Corner

Cornice
A projecting shelf along the top of a wall supported by ornamental brackets or a series of consoles.

Corona
The overhanging vertical member of a classical cornice supported by the bed moldings and crowned by the cymateum, usually incorporating a drip.

Cortile
An interior courtyard enclosed by the walls of a palace or other large building.

Court
An open space about which a building or several buildings are grouped, completely or partially enclosing the space. They may be roofed over with glass or open to the air.

Courtyard
An open area within the confines of other structures, sometimes as a semipublic space.

Crenellation
A pattern of repeated depressed openings in a fortification wall.

Crest
An ornament on a roof, a roof screen or wall, which is frequently perforated, and consists of rhythmic and identical patterns that are highly decorative.

Cupola
A tower-like device rising from the roof, usually terminating in a miniature dome or turret with a lantern or windows to let light in.

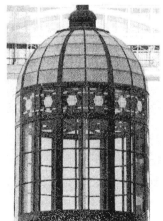

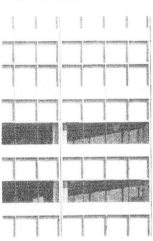

Curtain-wall
A method of construction in which all building loads are transmitted to a metal skeleton frame, so that the non-bearing exterior walls of metal and glass are simply a protective cladding.

Curtain wall

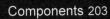

Dentil

An ornamental block resembling teeth, used as moldings often in continuous bands just below the cornice.

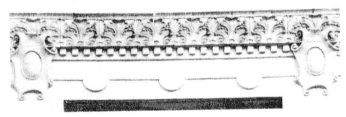

Dome

A curved roof structure that spans an area on a circular base, often hemispherical. A section can be semicircular, pointed or segmented.

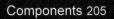

Bell-shaped dome
A dome whose cross-section is shaped in the form of a bell.

Geodesic dome
Consisting of a multiplicity of similar straight linear elements, arranged in triangles or pentagons, the members in tension having a minimal cross section, and making up a spherical surface usually in the shape of a dome.

Lattice dome
A steel dome structure having members which follow the circles of latitude *l* and two sets of diagonals replacing the lines of longitude and forming a series of isosceles triangles.

Melon dome
A melon-like ribbed dome, either on the interior or on the exterior.

Onion dome
In Russian Orthodox church architecture, a bulbous dome which terminates in a point and serves as a roof structure over a cupola or tower.

Radial dome
A dome built with steel or timber trusses arranged in a radial manner and connected by polygonal rings at various heights.

Semicircular dome
A dome in the shape of a half sphere.

Door

A hinged, sliding, tilting, or folding panel for closing openings in a wall or at entrances to buildings. Doors must relate to the facade or wall in which they are placed. They are an important element in setting the style of the exterior and are an important transitional element to the interior space.

Doorknocker

A knob, bar, or ring of metal, attached to the outside of an exterior door to enable a person to announce his or her presence, usually held by a hinge so that It can be lifted to strike a metal plate.

Door Surround
An ornamental border encircling the sides and top of a door frame.

Doorway
The framework in which the door hangs. or the entrance to a building. The doorway is the key area of interest in a facade as a natural focal point and design element giving human scale. The doorway also contains the street number.

Doorway

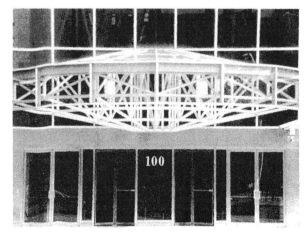

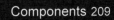

Doorway

Doorway

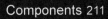

Doorway

Dormer
A structure projecting from a sloping roof usually housing a vertical window placed in a small gable or in a ventilating louver.

Dressing
Masonry and moldings of better quality than the facing materials, used around openings or at corners of buildings.

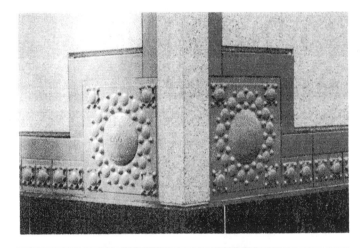

Entablature
The superstructure which lies above the columns in the architrave (immediately above the column), frieze (central part), and cornice (upper projecting mouldings).

Entasis
Intentional slight curvature given to the profile of a column to correct the optical illusion that it is thinner in the middle.

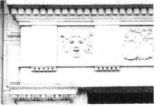

Entrance
Any passage that affords entry into a building; an exterior door, vestibule or lobby.

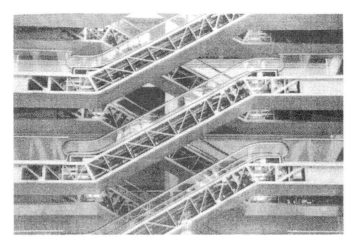

Escalator
A moving stairway consisting of steps attached to an inclined continuously moving belt for transporting passengers up or down between the floors in a structure.

Excavation
The removal of earth from its natural position; the cavity that results from the removal of earth.

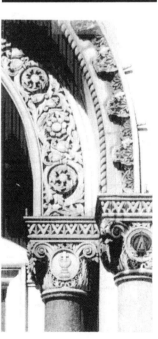

Extrados
The exterior curve or boundary on the visible face of the arch.

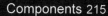

Facade
The main exterior face of a building, particularly one of its main sides, almost always containing an entrance and characterized by an elaboration of stylistic details.

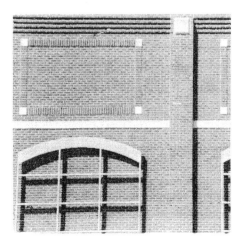

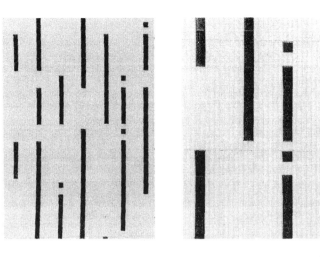

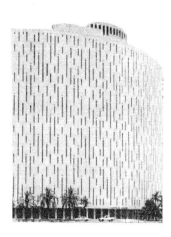

Fenestration

The design and placement of windows in a building. The number, shape and distribution of openings determines the character of the facade. Forms appear massive if the openings are relatively small, whereas large openings make the structure appear lighter.

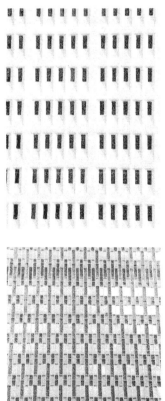

Fenestration

Festoon
Hanging clusters of fruit, tied in a bunch with leaves and flowers; used as decoration on pilasters and panels, usually hung between rosettes and skulls of animals.

Finial
An ornament at the top of a spire, pinnacle or gable which acts as a terminal

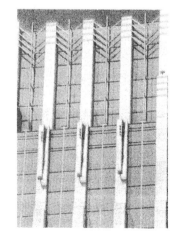

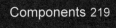

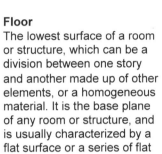

Floor

The lowest surface of a room or structure, which can be a division between one story and another made up of other elements, or a homogeneous material. It is the base plane of any room or structure, and is usually characterized by a flat surface or a series of flat surfaces at different levels.

Floor

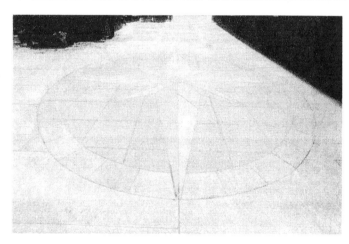

Floor

Flush Bead

An insert bead or convex molding, with its outer surface flush with adjacent surfaces.

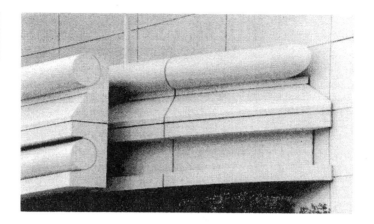

Fluting

The hollows or parallel channels cut vertically in the shape of columns, pilasters and piers. Some are separated by a sharp edge or arris, some by a small fillet.

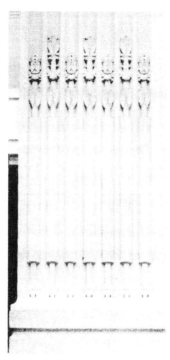

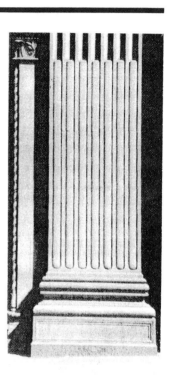

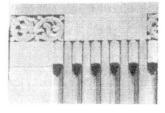

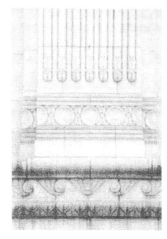

Foils
The foliation consists of the cusps, which are the projecting portions, and the spaces between the cusps.

Foliated
Adorned with foils, as on tracery; decorated with a conventionalized representation of leafage, applied to capitals, friezes, panels, or other ornamental moldings.

Fortress
A fortification of massive scale, generally of monumental character; sometimes including an urban core as a protected place of refuge.

Fountain
An architectural setting incorporating a continuous or artificial water supply, fed by a system of pipes and nozzles through which water is forced under pressure to produce a stream of ornamental jets.

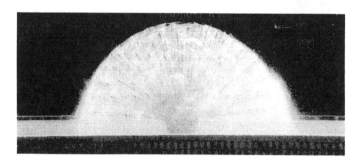

Fractable
A coping on the gable end of a building when carried above the roof, and broken into steps or curves forming an ornamental outline.

Fresco
A mural painted into freshly spread moist lime plaster; in such work, ground water-based pigments unite with the plaster base; retouching is done after it has dried.

Fretting
Decoration produced by cutting away the background of a pattern in stone or wood leaving the rest as grating.

Frieze
An elevated horizontal continuous band or panel, usually located below the cornice.

Gable

The entire triangular end of a wall, above the level of the eaves, the top of which conforms to the slope of the roof which abuts against it, sometimes stepped and sometimes curved in a scroll shape.

Gable

Garden

A piece of ground, open or enclosed, appropriated to plants, trees, shrubs, or other landscape features.

Gargoyle

A spout carrying water from the roofs above, frequently carved with grotesque figures or animals with open mouths, from which water is discharged away from the building's walls.

Gatehouse

A building, enclosing or accompanying a gateway for a castle, manor house, or similar building of importance.

Gateway

A passageway through a fence or wall; the structures at an entrance or gate designed for ornament or defense.

Gate tower

A tower containing a gate to a fortress.

Gazebo

A fanciful small structure, used as a summer house that is usually octagonal in plan with a steeply pitched roof that is topped by a finial. The sides are usually open, or latticed between the supports.

Gingerbread
The highly decorative wood-work applied to a Victorian style house.

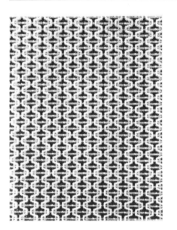

Grille
An ornamental arrangement of bars to form a screen or partition, usually of metal, wood, stone, or concrete, to cover, conceal, decorate, or protect an opening.

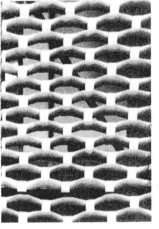

Grille

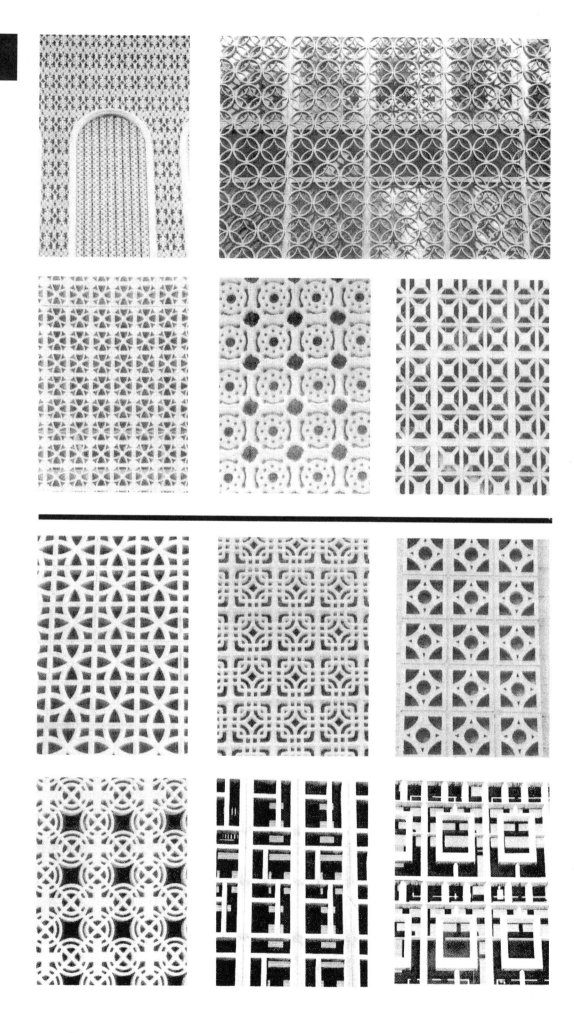

Groin
The curved area formed by the intersection of two vaults.

Groined rib
A rib under the curve of a groin, used as a device to either mask or support it.

Grotesque
Sculptured or painted ornament involving fanciful distortions of human and animal forms, sometimes combined with plant motifs, especially those without a counterpart in nature.

Grotto
A natural or artificial cave, often decorated with shells or stones and incorporating waterfalls or fountains.

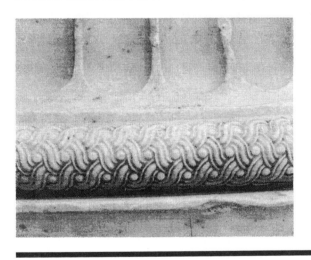

Guilloche
An ornament in the form of two or more bands twisted together in a continuous series, leaving circular openings that are filled with round ornaments.

Gutta
A small conical-shaped ornament resembling a droplet used in groups under the triglyph or the cornice found in Classical architecture.

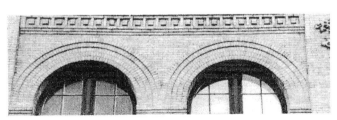

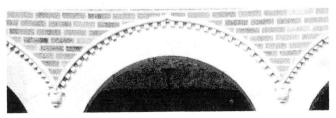

Haunch
The middle part of an arch, between the springing point and the crown.

Impost
The horizontal molding or
capital on top of a pilaster,
pier, or corbel which receives
and distributes the thrust at
the end of an arch.

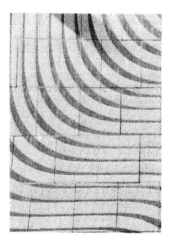

Intaglio
Incised carving in which the
forms are hollowed out of the
surface; the relief in reverse,
often used as a mold.

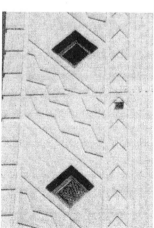

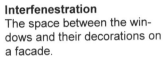

Interfenestration
The space between the windows and their decorations on a facade.

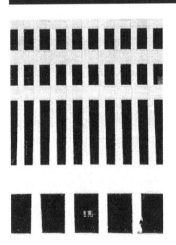

Interlaced Arches
Arches, usually circular, so
constructed that their forms
intersect each other.

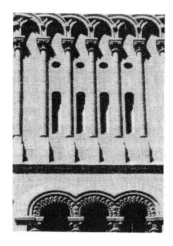

Interlaced Ornament
A band of ornamental figures
that are overlapped or intertwined to create resultant
forms.

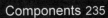

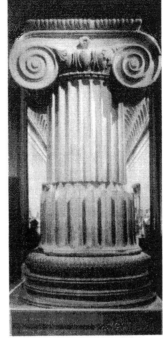

Ionic order

An order of architecture invented by the Greeks, distinguished by an elegantly molded base; tall, slender shafts with flutes separated by fillets; and capitals, using a spiral volute that supports an architrave with three fascias; an ornamental frieze, and a cornice corbeled out on egg-and-dart and dentil moldings.

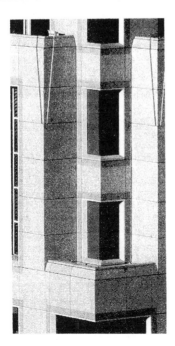

Jamb

The side of a window, door, chimney, or any other vertical opening.

Jamb shaft
A small shaft having a capital and a base, placed against the jamb of a door or window.

Joint
The space between the stones in masonry, or bricks in brickwork. In concrete work joints are necessary to allow the handling of conveniently sized areas, to allow shrinkage, and to ensure the isolation of independent elements. Control joints are tooled, sawed, or pre-molded, and installed to prevent shrinkage of large areas. They create a deliberately weakened section to induce cracking at the chosen location rather than at random.

Joint

Expansion joints are designed to permit the expansion or contraction due to temperature changes, and generally extends through the structure from the footings to the roof. Isolation joints separate one concrete section from another so that each one can move independently. They are often found in floors, at columns and at junctions between the floor and walls.

Keystone

The central stone or voissor at the top of the arch, the last part to be put into position to lock the arch in place, often embellished.

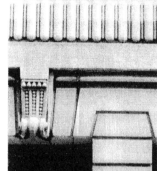

Kiosk

A small ornamented pavilion or gazebo, usually open for the sale of merchandise, or to provide cover or shelter to travelers.

Kneestone
A stone which is sloped on top and flat on the bottom that supports inclined coping on the side of a gable, or a stone that breaks the horizontal joint pattern to begin the curve of an arch.

Label stop
The termination of a hood-mold or arched dripstone in which the lower ends are turned in a horizontal direction away from the door or window opening.

Landmark
Any building structure or place that has a special character or special historic or aesthetic interest or value as part of the heritage or cultural character-istics of a city, state, or nation.

Lantern
A tower or small turret with windows, crowning a dome or cupola.

Lattice
A network of bars, straps, rods, or laths crossing over and under one another; the result is a rectangular or di-agonal checkered pattern , which may be varied by the width of the bands and the spacing of the members.

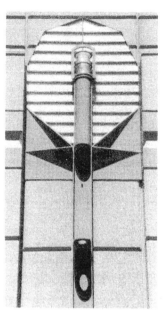

Light Fixture

A luminaire secured in place or attached as a permanent appendage or appliance. It consists of a lighting unit with lamps and components to protect the electrical circuits from the weather, and other devices to spread the light in a prescribed pattern.

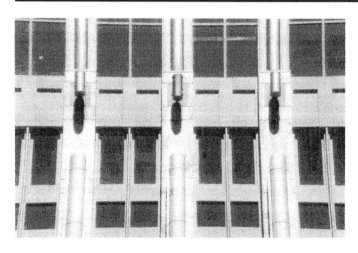

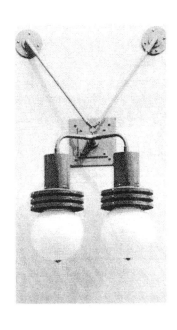

Light fixture

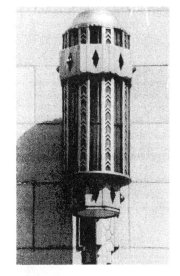

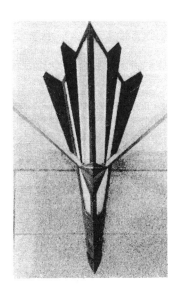

Light fixture

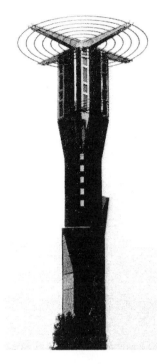

Louver
A window opening made of overlapping boards to ventilate without letting in the rain.

Lunette
A semicircular window or wall panel framed by an arch or vault.

Machicolation
Openings formed by setting the parapets out on corbels so as to project beyond the face of the wall. Some para-. pets set out on corbels have a similar appearance, even if there are no openings.

Medallion
An ornamental plaque with an object in relief, applied to a wall or frieze.

Molding
A decorative profile given to architectural members and sub-ordinate parts of buildings, whether cavities or projections, such as cornices, bases, or door and window jambs and heads.

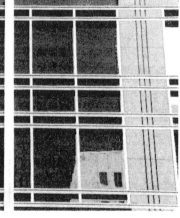

Mullion
A dividing piece between the lights of windows, taking on the characteristics of the style of the building.

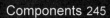

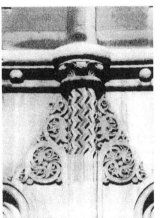

Niche
A recess in a wall, usually semi-circular at the back, terminating in a half-dome, or with small pediments supported on consoles; most often used as a place for a statue.

Ornament
Anything that embellishes, decorates, or adorns a structure, whether used intentionally and integrated into the structure, or applied for the sake of enhancing the buildings' form and appearance. The ornament can be limited to the structural elements only, such as pinnacles and buttresses. The structure can become an ornament, such as the appearance of structural bracing forms on the surface. Certain structural elements can be used ornamentally, such as exposed curtain wall sections. Ornament that is applied is generally unrelated to the structure, and exists for its own sake.

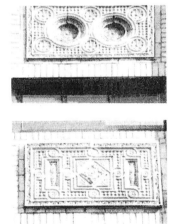

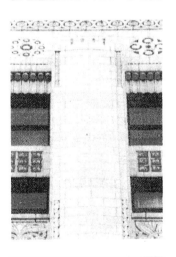

Ornament

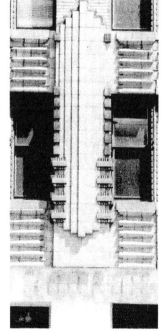

Ornament

Overhang
The horizontal distance that the upper story or roof projects beyond the story immediately below.

Panel
A portion of a flat surface recessed below the surrounding area, set off by moldings or some other distinctive feature.

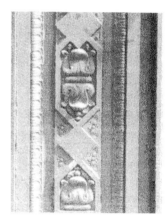

Parapet
A low protective wall or railing along the edge of a raised platform, terrace, bridge, roof, balcony, and above cornices, Where it is used as an architectural feature it is often decorated and incorporated Into the design composition.

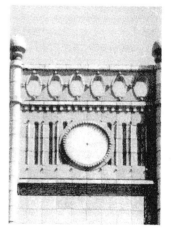

Pavilion

An open structure or small ornamental building, shelter or kiosk used as a summer house or as an adjunct of a larger building. It is usually a detached structure for specialized activities, and is often located as a terminal structure with a hipped roof on all sides so as to have a pyramidal form.

Pendant

A hanging ornament or suspended feature on ceilings or vaults.

Pendentive

The curved triangular surface that results when the top corner of a square space is vaulted so as to provide a circular base for a dome.

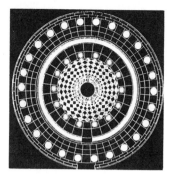

Peristyle
A row of columns around the outside of a building or around the inside of a court- yard.

Pier
A free-standing support for an arch, usually composite in section and thicker than a column, but performing the same function; also, a thick- ened part of a wall to provide lateral support or take con- centrated loads.

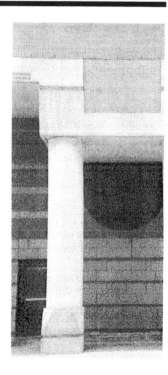

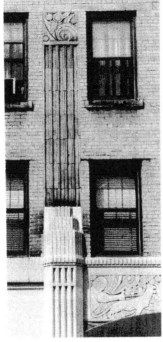

Pilaster
A partial pier or column, often with a base and capital that is embedded in a flat wall and projects slightly.

Pinnacle
An apex or small turret that usually tapers towards the top as a termination to a buttress.

Plaza
An open square or market place having one or more levels, approached in various ways by avenues, streets, or stairs or a combination.

Portal
An entrance, gate, or door to a building or courtyard, that is often decorated, which marks the transition from the public exterior to the private interior space.

Portico
A range of columns in front of a building, often merged into the facade, including a covered walkway of which one or more sides are open.

Pylon.
A monumental gateway in the form of a truncated pyramid or other vertical shaft that marks the entrance approach to a structure.

Relief
Sculptural decoration in low relief, in which none of the figures or motifs are separated from their background, projecting less than half their true proportions from the wall or surface. When the projection is equal to half the true proportion *it* is called mezzo-relievo; when more than half. it is alto relievo. Double-aspect sculpture is that which is halfway between relief and sculpture-in-the-round.

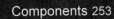

Relief

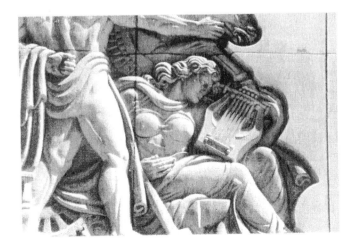

Relief

Reticulated Work
Masonry constructed with diamond-shaped stones, or square stones placed diagonally or crossing in a network.

Reveal
The visible side of an opening for a window or doorway between the framework and outer surface of the wall; where the opening is not filled with a door or window, the whole thickness of the wall.

Roof
The external covering on the top of a building, usually of wood shingles, slates, or tiles on pitched slopes, or a variety of built-up membranes for flat roofs.

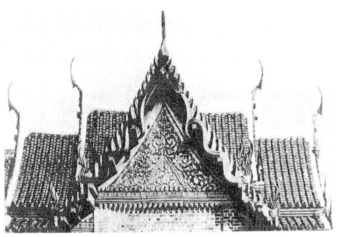

Barrel roof
A roof of semi-cylindrical section: capable of spanning long distances, parallel to the axis of the cylinder.

Bell roof
A roof whose cross section is shaped like a bell.

Curb roof
A pitched roof that slopes away from the ridge in two successive planes, as in a gambrel or mansard roof.

Gable roof
A roof having a gable at one or both ends: a roof sloping downward in two opposite directions from a central ridge, so as to form a gable at each end.

Gambrel roof
A roof which has two pitches on each side.

Mansard roof
A roof with a steep lower slope and a flatter upper slope on all sides, either of convex or concave shape.

Ogee roof
A roof whose section is an ogee.

Pavilion roof
A roof hipped equally on all sides, so as to have a pyramidal form; a similar roof having more than four sides, a polygonal roof.

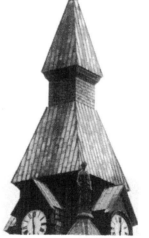

Pent roof

A small sloping roof, the upper end of which butts against a wall of a house, usually above the first-floor window; if carried completely around the house, it is called a skirt roof.

Pitched roof

A roof having one or more slopes, surfaces.

Pyramidal hipped roof

Same as a pavilion roof.

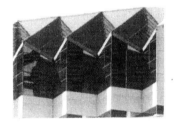

Sawtooth roof

A roof system having a number of small parallel roof surfaces with a profile similar to the teeth in a saw; usually the steeper side is splayed and faces north; usually asymmetrical with the shorter slope glazed.

Stepped roof

A roof constructed of stones which are arranged in a stair-stepped fashion, diminishing towards the top in a peak.

Suspended roof

One whose load is carried by a number of cables which are under tension from columns or posts that are in compression and that transmit the loads to the ground.

Thatched roof

A roof made of straw, reed, or similar materials fastened together to shed water and sometimes to provide thermal insulation.

Rotunda
A building that is round both inside and outside, usually covered with a dome.

Rustication
Masonry cut in large blocks with the surface left rough and unfinished, separated by deep recessed joints. The border of each block may be beveled or rabeted on all four sides or top and bottom. It is used mainly on the lower part of a structure to give a bold , exaggerated took of strength.

Scaffold
A temporary platform to support workers and materials on the face of a structure and to provide access to work areas above the ground; any elaborated platform.

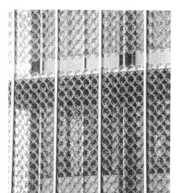

Screen facade
A nonstructural facing assembly used to disguise the form or overall size of a building.

Scroll
An ornamental molding consisting of a spiral design; or a terminal like the volutes of the Ionic capital, or the S curves on consoles.

Section
The representation of a building or portion thereof, cut vertically at some imagined plane, so as to show the interior of the space or the profile of the member.

Section

Shaft

The main body of a column, pilaster or pier between the capital and the base, or a thin vertical member attached to a wall or pier, often supporting an arch or vaulting rib.

Shafting

In medieval architecture, an arrangement of shafts, combined in the mass of a pier or jamb, so that corresponding groupings of archivolt moldings above may start from their caps at the impost line.

Skewback

The sloping surface of a member which receives the component materials of an arch.

Skylight

An opening in a roof which is glazed with a transparent or translucent material used to admit natural or diffused light to the space below.

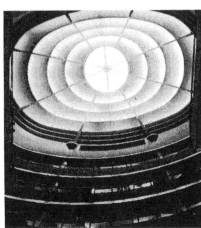

Soffit

A ceiling or exposed under-side surface of entablatures, archways, balconies, beams, lintels or columns.

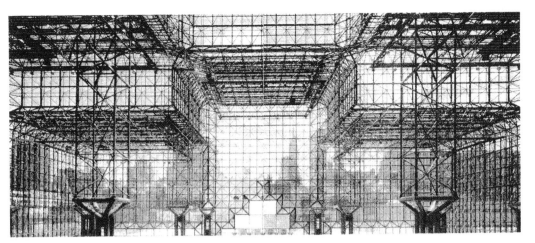

Space Frame
A three-dimensional structural framework made up of interconnected triangular elements that enclose a space; as opposed to a frame where all the elements lie in a single plane.

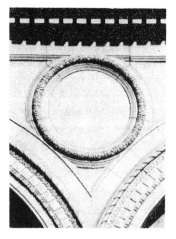

Spandrel

The triangular space formed between the sides of adjacent arches and the line across their tops. In a skeletal frame building it consists of the walls inside the columns and between the top of the window of one story and the sill of the window above.

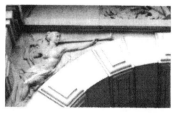

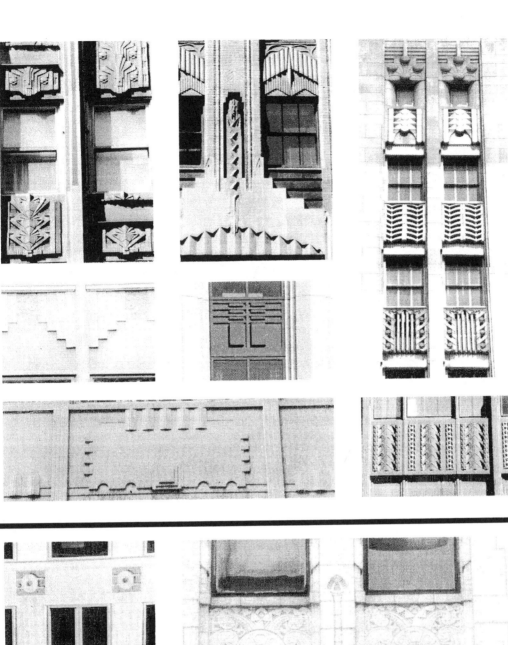

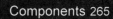
Spandrel panel
A panel covering the spandrel area between the head of a window on one level and the sill of the window immediately above.

Stair

A series of steps or flights of steps for traveling between two or more successive levels with connecting landings at each level, either on the exterior or interior.

Staircase

A vertical element of access in a structure for ascending or descending from one level to another. The form of the staircase is often expressed on the exterior of the building, if it is located adjacent to an exterior wall.

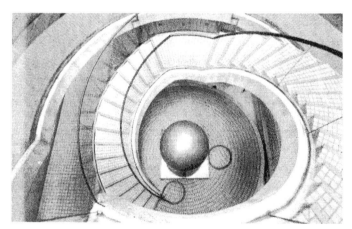

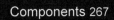

Steel Frame
A skeleton of steel beams and columns providing all that is structurally necessary for the building to stand.

Steel Frame

Symbol
Something that stands for or represents something else by association, resemblance, or convention, deriving its meaning chiefly from the structure on which it appears.

Terminal
A terminus occurring at the end of a series of incidents, such as an ornamental figure or object situated at the end of something such as a finial.

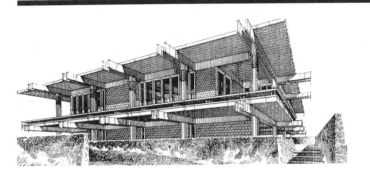

Trabeation
Construction using upright posts and horizontal beams and lintels, rather than arches or vaults.

Trellis
A structural frame supporting an open latticework or grating constructed of either metal or wood, used to support plants or vines or left exposed.

Trellis

Triglyph
A grooved tablet in the frieze of the Doric Order, with three vertical V-shaped channels or flutes separated by two narrow flat spaces, occurring over the center of columns.

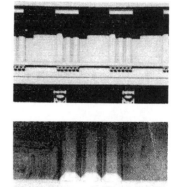

Turret
A diminutive tower, characteristically projecting out on corbels from a corner of the structure.

Tympanum
The triangular space between the horizontal and sloping cornices, immediately above the opening of a doorway.

Vault
An arched roof in a continuous semicircular ceiling that extends in a straight line.

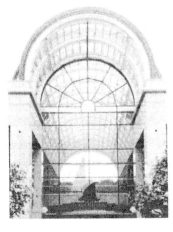

Voussoir
A wedge-shaped block whose converging sides radiate from the center forming an element of an arch or vaulted ceiling.

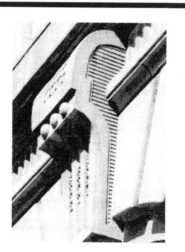

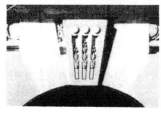

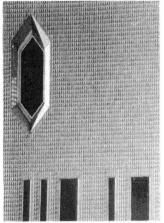

Window
An exterior wall opening, usually glazed, admitting light and air, fitted with the assembly of window frame, glazing, and operable elements. These operable windows are identified by the way they work; double hung, casement, sliding, pivoting, and louvered.

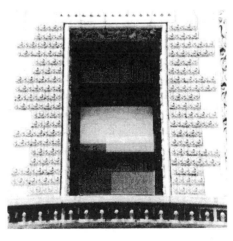

Window

Window

Bay window
A window forming a recess in a room and projecting outwards from the wall either in a rectangular, polygonal or semi-circular form. Some are supported on corbels or on projecting moldings.

Blank window
A recess in an exterior wall, having the external appearance of a window; a window which has been sealed off but is still visible.

Camber window
A window arched at the top.

Cant window
A bay window erected on a plan of canted outlines; the sides are not at right angles to the wall.

Coupled window
Two closely spaced windows which form a pair.

Dormer window
A vertical window that projects from a sloping roof, placed in a small gable.

Double-hung window
A window having two vertically sliding sashes, each closing a different part of the window; the weight of each sash is counterbalanced for ease of opening and closing.

Double window
Two windows, side by side, which form a single architectural unit.

False window
The representation of a window that is inserted into a facade to complete a series of windows or to give the appearance of symmetry.

Gable window
A window in a gable; a window shaped like a gable.

Lancet window
A narrow window with a sharp pointed arch that is typical of English Gothic architecture; one light shaped in the form of a lancet window.

Lucarne window
A small dormer window in a roof or spire. -

Oriel window
A bay window corbeled out from a wall of an upper story; a projecting bay that forms the extension of a room, used extensively in medieval English residential architecture.

Ox-eye window
A round or oval aperture, open, louvered, or glazed; an occulus or oeil-de-boeuf.

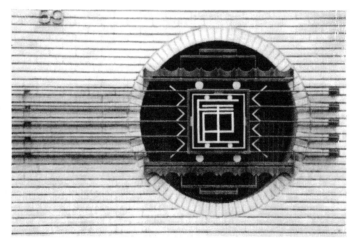

Ox-eye window

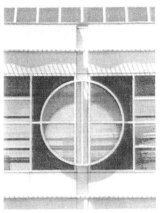

Ribbon window
One of a horizontal series of
windows, separated only by
mullions, which forms a horizontal band across the facade
of a building.

Rose window
A large, circular medieval
window, containing tracery
disposed in a radial manner.

Roundel
A small circular panel or window; an oculus, a bull's eye or
circular light like the bottom of
a bottle.

Stained-glass window
A window whose glass is colored.

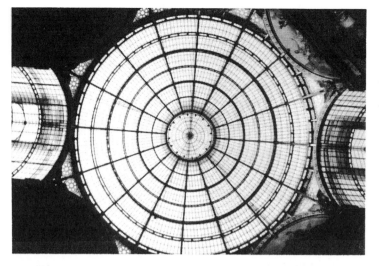

Wheel window
A large circular window in which the tracery radiates from the center; a variety of the rose window.

Window casing
The finished frame surrounding a window; the visible frame; usually consists of wood, metal, or stone.

Window Frame
The fixed, non-operable frame of a window, consisting of two jambs, a head and a sill, designed to receive and hold the sash or casement and all necessary hardware.

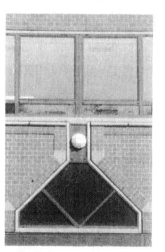

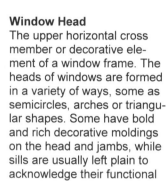

Window Head
The upper horizontal cross member or decorative element of a window frame. The heads of windows are formed in a variety of ways, some as semicircles, arches or triangular shapes. Some have bold and rich decorative moldings on the head and jambs, while sills are usually left plain to acknowledge their functional aspect of shedding water.

Window head

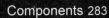

Window Head

Window Head

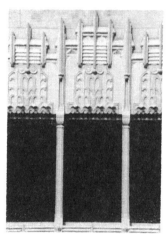
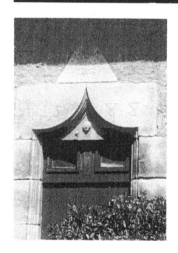

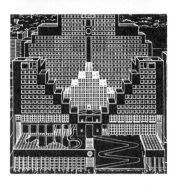

Architecture can give us insight into the nature of our own culture because it is so bound up with the life of the culture as a whole. It reflects the conditions of the period from which it springs, from the fondness for certain shapes and forms to the approaches to specific building problems. It is the product of social, economic and technological factors. One fact is indisputable; every architectural form and building element has evolved over eons of time from the use of raw materials in early buildings. Architectural forms were a combination of art and utility, and they show the human creative impulse inherent in the design of structures.

The forms characteristic of the various architectural styles are intimately related to the systems of construction and the materials used during any one period. The expression of these forms differs considerably from one region to the next, and from one historic period to the next. The structurally inert forms of Persia, Mesopotamia and Egypt are characterized by surface decoration unrelated to the structural function of the bearing members. In Egypt, for example, the column was shaped as a decorative element first and as a structural member second. In Crete the columns were separate elements which tapered downwards, which is generally regarded as a form that expresses its function, which is of course the transfer of loads. In Greek architecture the column was more deliberately expressed as an active element of the load-bearing system. In post-and-beam construction it became a central theme and contributed to the modular system that grew out of the classical orders. The shapes of classical building elements, columns, capitals, base moldings and the like all indicate a transfer of loads.

In Roman architecture the arch and the vault enormously enlarged the scope of building and allowed much more expansive spaces. The vault and dome were known in the ancient Near East, but it was the Romans who realized their full structural possibilities and applied them to architecture. This type of construction became the dominant theme in Byzantine, Romanesque and Gothic architecture. The forms of these works reveal how forces balance, how they change direction, and how loads are transferred to the ground.

In Gothic architecture creative expression was inspired by the art of transferring forces. Inside a cathedral one cannot see the buttresses that receive the thrusts. From the outside their form is clearly expressed. The technical innovations of the Gothic style came entirely from the architecture itself, by enabling buildings to be built on a skeletal framework. An overall geometric pattern was fundamental to the design of cathedrals.

Renaissance architectural form in many ways is similar to Roman form in which the ultimate goal was a harmonious composition of the geometrical shapes of the facade. To this end, columns, architraves, pediments, arches, pilasters and piers are combined regardless of whether they correspond to the structural integrity of the building or not. During the Renaissance there was a tendency to express forces by means of building forms. In Baroque architecture, space expressed movement in excessive undulating forms.

Another aesthetic property of form is harmony of shape. These forms derive their appeal from the laws of geometry. Seen from the outside, a building appears as a volume or as a combination of different volumes, horizontal or vertical, compact or spread out. Whereas exterior space is undefined, interior space is made up of volume defined by the architectural shell. One must differentiate between what is due to structural necessities, stylistic conventions, or materials limitations, and what is the product of purely artistic creation, the play of forms.

Modernism was the first style that did not permit eclecticism. All previous cultures dipped into the past reservoir of ornamental elements and architectural forms. Since there is no absolute standard in the arts, the nineteenth century architects who thought that certain forms were valid for every age were certainly mistaken. The modern designer had to reinvent ornamental form. It now had to look as if it belonged to the building. Many of today's architects still have a form vocabulary composed mainly of geometric and structural elements. It has not changed in over a century,despite numerous examples of free sculptural form by experimental architects.

In the twentieth century the development of technology made the construction of high-rise buildings possible through the use of a steel frame. The developments that followed have been primarily in the materials to cover this frame, such as metals, glass, precast panels and cut stone cladding. In this new prototype of the multistory office building the load-bearing frame is concealed and a fully glazed outer skin forms a curtain wall. With its precise rectilinear shape free of all decoration, this building type proved to be the starting point of a new direction in architectural form. The walls, which are not load-bearing consist of pressed aluminum panels or prefabricated materials assembled for easy on-site installation. Verticals and horizontals are distributed in many different ways in the treatment of the glass facade. The division by stories is clearly shown, and sometimes the structural frame is visible through the transparent planes. More recent buildings play decorative tricks with these curtain walls, particularly with the use of reflective glass panels. This building form spawned a stock of forms which could be characterized by transparency, visual lightness and apparent weightlessness.

The excessively smooth form of the curtain-wall forms are contrasted by the rugged forms of other examples. In certain structures the wall becomes heavy and solid even when it is not load-bearing. Building materials have rough, granular and contrasting textures such as brick and exposed concrete. Acute or obtuse angles are the norm, with hard, dissonant articulation of the individual building parts. The visual scale consists of small units abruptly confronted with larger ones. The overall form is heavy in appearance.

Modern architecture, which ostensibly created an original style, repeatedly borrowed from its own past over and over again. In later Postmodern styles there is also constant borrowing from other styles. Contemporary architecture, however, demanded honesty in the outward appearance of materials and construction techniques. It has led to new forms that express in a more direct way the structural qualities that derives from new techniques. Forms must conform more directly to the system of construction, and must clearly and consistently express the materials used. Whatever happens beyond that is the direct result of the creative talent of the designer, who must find a way to design the ultimate form of the building as one that transcends all other considerations to become a true work of art.

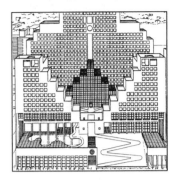

Form:

The contour and structure of an object as distinguished from its substance, or from the matter composing it; its distinctive appearance as determined by its visible lines, figure, outline, configuration and profile.
(from Latin forma; *form, contour.*)

Amorphous

Amorphous forms are those that do not have a definite or specific shape, or a distinctive crystalline, geometric, angular or curvilinear structure.

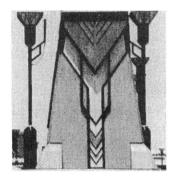

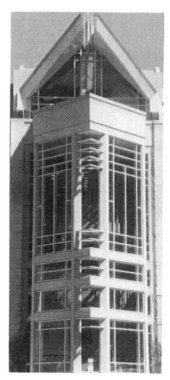

Angular

Angular figures are formed by two lines diverging from a common point, two planes diverging from a common line, and the space between such lines or surfaces, whether on the exterior or interior of a structure.

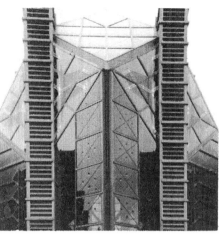

Angular

Arched

Arched shapes are formed by the curved, pointed, or rounded upper part of openings or supporting members.

Arched

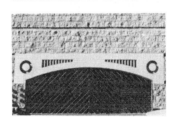

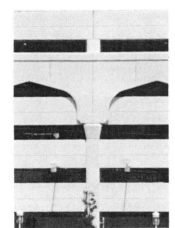

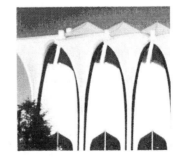

Arched

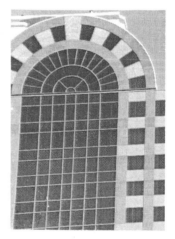

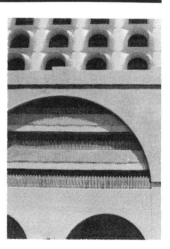

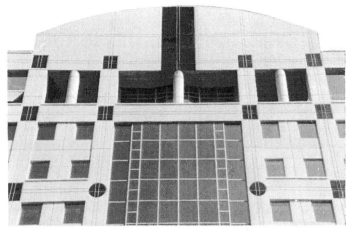

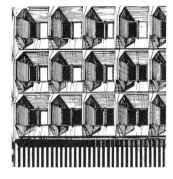

Articulated

Articulated shapes are those having joints or segments which subdivide the surface. The joints or members add scale and rhythm to an otherwise plain surface.

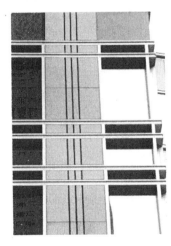

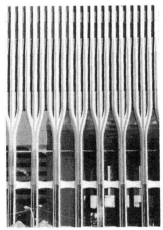

Battered

Battered forms slope from a true vertical plane from bottom to top, as in the outside suface of a wall.

Beveled

A bevel is a sloped or canted surface resembling a splay or chamfer, where the sides are sloped for the purpose of enlarging or reducing them.

A cant occurs when any part of a building has the corners cut off at an angle to the square. This applies to windows, balconies, corners and bays, as well as to details and ornamental panels.

Beveled

Form 296

 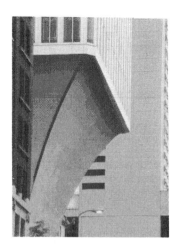 

Cantilevered

Forms that are cantilevered have rigid structural members or walls projecting significantly beyond their vertical support.

Chamfered

A chamfer is a flat surface made by cutting off the edge or corner, as in a beveled or canted form.

Checkered

Checkered forms are those that are marked off with a pattern of checks or squares that is divided into different colors, or variegated by a checked or square pattern of different materials.

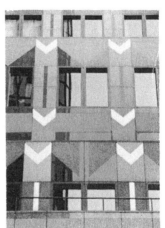

Chevron

A chevron is a symmetrical "V" shape that represents a triangle with its third side removed. The chevron can be bordered, inter-laced and repeated in various patterns, pointing up or down. It can be used singly or in groups. It has always been a widely used motif in surface decoration, even in the most modern buildings, although it had a much wider use in the Art Deco period.

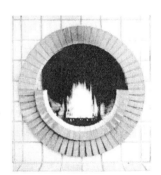

Circular

The circular form occurs frequently in nature, and has been used since the earliest of times to represent the sun and the moon. Since it is without a beginning or end, the circle has always been the symbol of eternity, completeness and perfection.

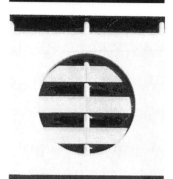

Circular

The circle is the simplest and most fundamental of all geometric shapes. It is defined as a continuous curved line, every point of which is equidistant from a central point. It forms the basis of an infinite number of shapes, forms and patterns. By using the process of subdivision and interlacement, it is possible to produce an endless variety of forms. The subdivision of the circle is accomplished by straight lines, arcs, or any combination of the two. A segment of a circle occurs inside its outline.

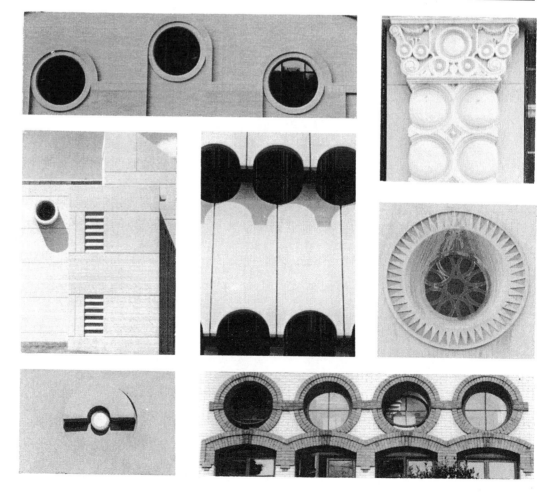

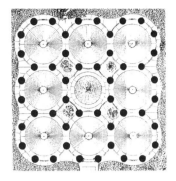

Circular

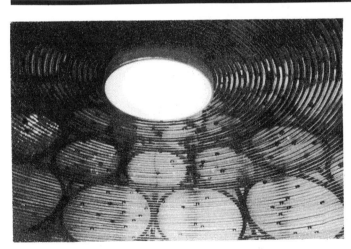

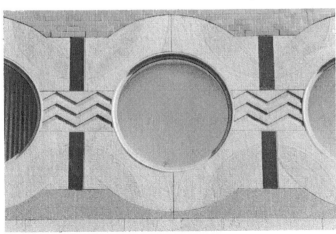

Circular

Cityscape

This is represented by the silhouette of groups of urban structures that make up a skyline. It may include distinguished landmarks, natural and built. These would include steeples of churches, spires, water towers, cupolas and domes, tops of buildings, and natural elements such as rolling hills, mountains or large bodies of water.

Cluster

Clustered forms are derived from any configuration of elements that are grouped or are gathered closely together.

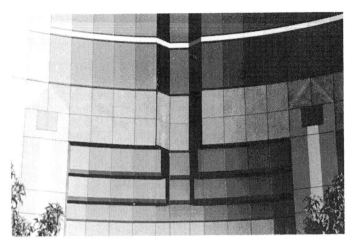

Form 301

Concave
Concave forms are curved like the inner surface of a sphere.

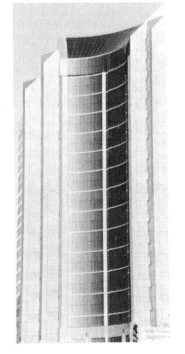

Conical
Pertaining to a cone shape.

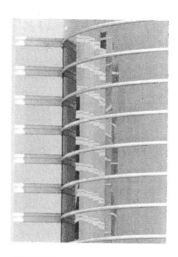

Convex

Convex forms have a surface or boundary that curves outward, as in the exterior or outer surface of a sphere.

Corrugated

Shaped into folds of parallel and alternating ridges and valleys either to provide additional strength, or to vary the surface pattern.

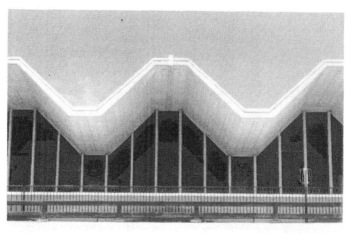

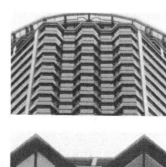

Cross

When two lines intersect each other at right angles so that the four arms are equal length, the resultant form is the cross. A very common variation of this form is the extension of one of the arms to a length greater than the other three. This is the form of the cross that was adopted by the Roman church, whereas one with four equal arms was adopted by the Greek church.

Crystalline

A crystal is a three-dimensional structure consisting of periodically repeated, identically constituted, congruent unit cells. Crystalline forms are found in abundance in natural objects.

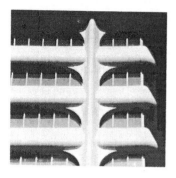

Form 304

Curvilinear

These forms are not necessarily derivative of the circle, but are formed, bounded, or characterized by curved lines, whether they are geometric or free flowing.

Curvilinear

Cylindrical
Having the shape of a cylinder.

Form 306

Cylindrical

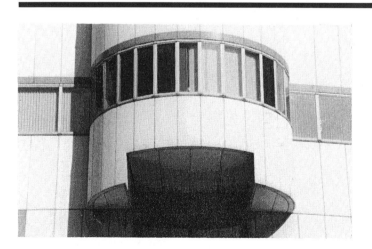

Cylindrical

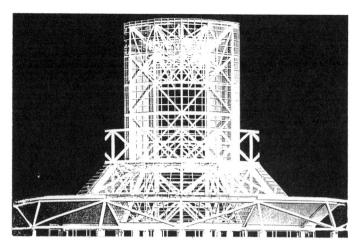

Diagonal

A diagonal joins two non-adjacent sides of a polygon, and has a slanted or oblique direction from one corner to the other. Their use in a square or rectangle produces two triangular shapes.

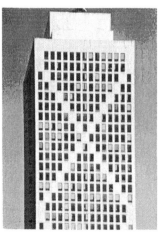

Diagonal

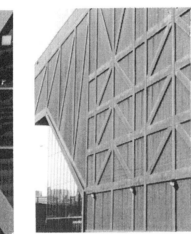

Diamond Fret

This describes a molding that is usually continuous, consisting of fillets that intersect to form a diamond shape.

Diaper Patterns

These are flat patterns based on grids, but the patterns can contain either straight or curved lines. The grid may overlap or produce figures by connecting the diagonals and combining them with circles, arcs and segments. The designs may be useful for flooring, tilework or window glazing.

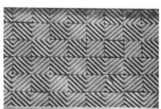

Elliptical

The ellipse is a plane figure whose radius of curvature is continually changing. The three-centered arch is an appropriate construction to an elliptical curve.

Faceted

Faceted shapes resemble any of the flat, angular surfaces cut on a gemstone.

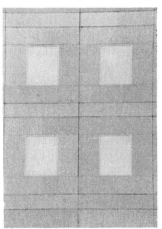

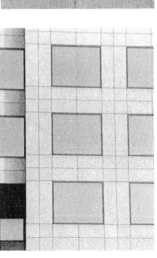

Flush

This signifies that the adjoining surfaces in a building or in a wall are even, level, or arranged so that their edges are close together and on the same plane.

Form 312

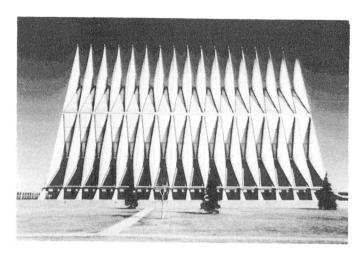

Folded Plates

The accordion shapes in this type of structural system consist of a series of folded plates, introduced into the roof slabs to provide additional stiffness, and to protect against surface buckling. The plates are hinged with rigid joints along their common edges. These lightweight forms can span substantial distances, and they are usually expressed on the facade as a design element.

Framework

A framework is composed of individual parts that are fitted and joined together. They are skeletal structures designed to produce a specific shape, or to provide temporary or permanent support.

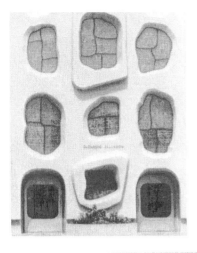

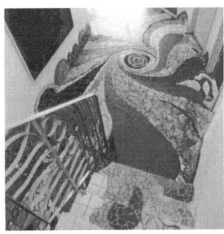

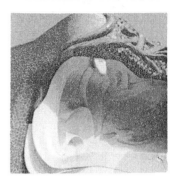

Freeform

Freeform shapes are characterized by a free flowing rather than a geometric structure. They usually resemble forms found in nature.

Geodesic

Geodesic forms are grid structures that consist of a multiplicity of similar straight linear elements, arranged in triangles or pentagons. They are arranged structurally so that the members are usually in tension and have a minimal cross section. They make up a spherical surface, usually in the shape of a dome.

Geometrical

Geometrical forms relate to the properties of geometry, such as those forms that can be generated by plane figures into three-dimensional forms. Geometric forms encompass the whole range of buildings from overall shape, contour, outline, detail and ornament.

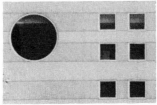

Grids

A grid consists of a framework of parallel, crisscrossed lines or bars forming a pattern of uniform size. Grids consist of sets of intersecting members on a square or triangular matrix, which make up a three-dimensional structural system. Grids may employ trusses, or composite systems combined to form larger grid structures. Their main characteristic is strength relative to the size of the members incorporated in the grid.

Hexagonal

A hexagon is a plane geometric figure containing six equal sides and angles. Hexagonal forms are widely used because of their occurrence in nature as minerals, honeycombs, and snow crystals.

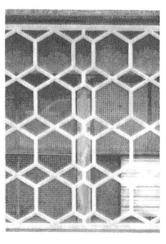

Hollow Sections

A box girder is a hollow beam with either a square, rectangular or circular cross section. These forms are sometimes vertical instead of horizontal, and are attached firmly to the ground like cantilevers. Such structural systems include tall buildings with facade trusses and an invisible central stiffening core. The horizontal hollow section forms tend to be expressed more prominently and give the appearance of sturdiness and stability.

Hyperbolic / Paraboloid

All hyperbolic / paraboloid shapes are convoluted in two directions, as opposed to arched or vaulted ones. They have a surface in which all sections parallel to one coordinate plane are hyperbolas, and all sections parallel to the other plane are parabolas. Both hyperbolas and parabolas are conic sections.

Interlaced

Intermixed forms that cross over each other with alternation as if woven together are interlaced.

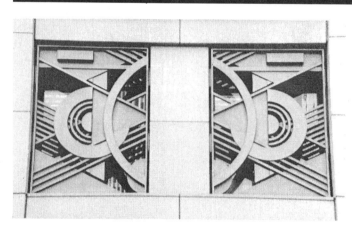

Interlocking
Interlocked forms are united firmly or joined closely by hooking or dovetailing.

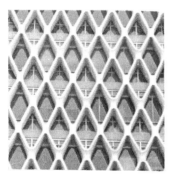

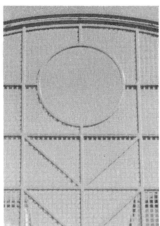

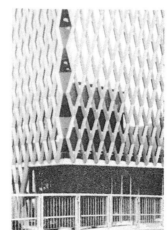

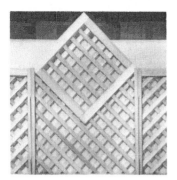

Lattice

The lattice or basket weave is the result of bands crossing over and under one another. The result is a rectangular or diagonal checkered pattern, which may be varied by the width of the bands and the spacing and alternation of the members. Latticed forms are used as screening or airy ornamental construction.

Lozenge

A lozenge is an equilateral four-sided figure with pairs of equal angles; two acute and two obtuse. The main characteristic is that of a rhombic or diamond-shaped figure. The principle auxiliary lines of the figure are the diagonals. The subdivision generally leaves an oblong or hexagonal panel in the center.

Lozenge

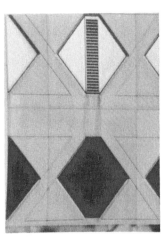

Membranes

A great variety of shapes belong in the family of membranes, including air-supported structural forms. There are two types: forms that include nets filled with a membrane, and forms with a fabric surface. The characteristic shape is like an elastic membrane.

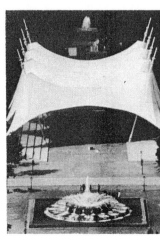
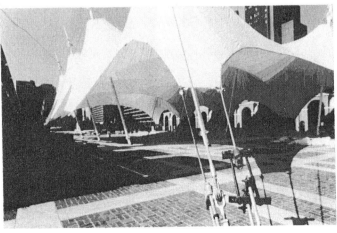

Monolithic

Monolithic shapes are usually formed of a single block of stone. They are massive and uniform. Concrete cast in one piece without construction joints is an example of monolithic construction.

Octagonal

The octagon is a plane geometric figure containing eight equal sides and angles. Of all the many-sided polygons, it is next to the hexagon in terms of use as a design element. It was one of the favorite forms of the Romans and found its way into the plan designs of many early churches. It was also a favorite form for towers and other ancillary spaces. It is still in wide use today.

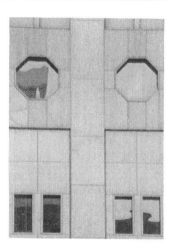

Ornamental

Ornamental forms are those that adorn or embellish a surface or any other part of a structure. Before modernism, almost all buildings had some form of ornamentation. It was seldom thought of as something separate from architectural form. This unity of the architecture and ornament could encompass virtually every part of a building.

Oval

Oval-shaped spaces are not a modification of circular spaces, but an independent type which has always been seen in contrast to the circle. The circle is mono-centric, the oval duo-centric with a long and short axis.

Overhanging

An overhang projects or extends beyond the wall surface below.

Overlapping

Overlapping forms extend over and cover part of an area or surface that has a common alignment. The overlap may be slight or it may be significant, as long as they have a common surface between them.

Plaid

The plaid is a pattern created by regularly spaced bands at right angles to one another. The resultant checkered effects can vary widely, depending on the relationship and intervals between lines and bands.

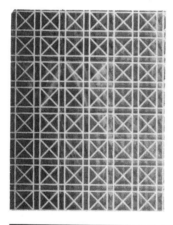

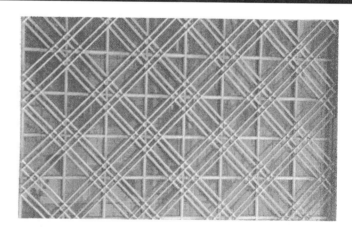

Post-and-Beam

The forms resulting from this structural system date back to the beginning of construction. More or less complex variants of this system are used today. The forms of simple one-story structures express the post-and-beam in straightforward ways. In many poured concrete structures the posts and beams are all interconnected to form multistoried skeleton frames.

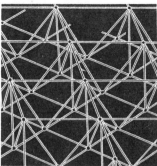

Prismatic

A prism is a solid figure of which the two ends are similar figures with parallelograms for sides. Prismatic forms are found in space frames covering open areas.

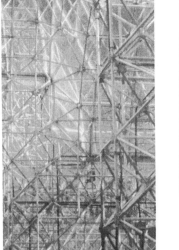

Pyramidal

A pyramid is a polyhedron with a rectangular base and four triangular faces meeting at a single common apex. Pyramidal forms are among the oldest in recorded history, and are used extensively to this day to form space frames and other triangulated elements.

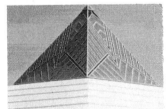

Form 324

Pyramidal

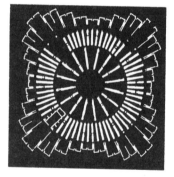

Radial

This applies to forms radiating from or converging to a common center, or developing symmetrically about a central point.

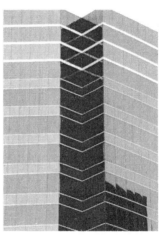

Recessed

Recessed forms are created by indentations or small hollows in an otherwise plain surface or straight line. Recesses can be angular, rectilinear or curvilinear.

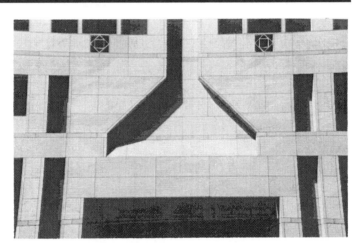

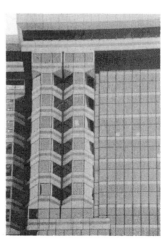

Rectangular

A rectangle is a plane four-sided parallelogram with four right angles. It may be nearly square or stretched out to be nearly a band. The "Golden Section" was a rectangle, one whose proportions were said to be perfectly harmonious, and in keeping with other laws of nature.

Relief

Architecture has nearly always been embellished with sculpture and bas-relief ornamentation in every imaginable material from delicate wood and terracotta to more durable limestone, marble, granite, and metals such as copper and bronze.

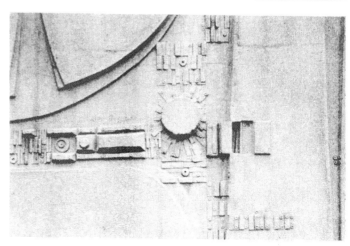

Reticulated

Reticulated work refers to surfaces that are marked with lines, resembling or forming a network of squares set on the diagonal.

Rotated

Rotated forms are created by revolving a shape on an axis and duplicating it in another location with the same relationship to the central point.

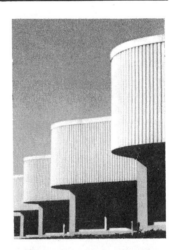

Rounded

Rounded forms may be spherical, globular, shaped like a ball, or circular in cross section.

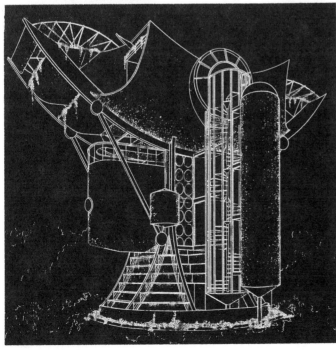
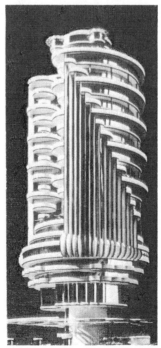

Rounded

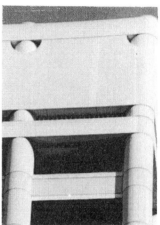

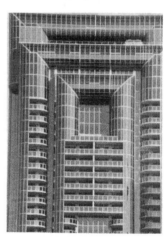

Scroll

A scroll is ornamentation that consists of a spirally wound band or resembles a partially rolled scroll of paper, especially in the volute in the Ionic and Corinthian capitals. "S" scrolls are found in ornamental brackets, window and door surrounds, and in other ornamental bands.

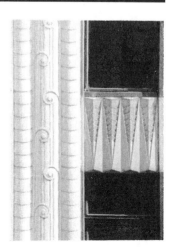

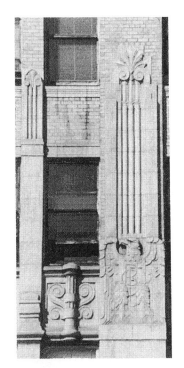

Scroll

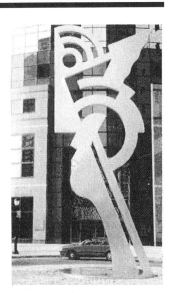

Sculpture

Sculpture is the art of shaping figures, forms, or designs by carving wood, chiseling marble, modeling clay, or casting in metal. In architecture, sculptural forms can be achieved through a variety of materials; including brick, stone, and concrete.

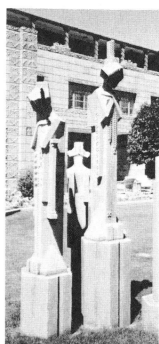

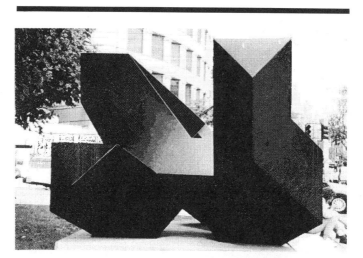

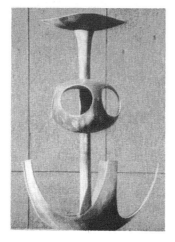

Sculpture

Shells

Shells are hollow structures in the form of thin curved slabs, plates or membranes which are self supporting. Shells are called "form resistant structures" because they are shaped according to the loads they carry.

Spherical

A sphere is a three-dimensional surface, all parts of which are equidistant from a fixed point.

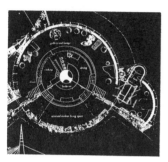

Spiral

Spiral forms are generated by a continuous curve traced by a point moving around a fixed point in a fixed plane, while steadily increasing the distance from the point. Another term for the spiral is the helix, which is generated in the same manner.

Splayed

An oblique slope given to the sides of an opening in a wall so that the opening is wider at one face than the other. This also applies to any exterior wall surface that is slanted or sloped in any direction from true vertical.

Square

A square is a regular four-sided figure with equal sides and all right angles. It is a fundamental form. It may be subdivided in various ways. The principle auxiliary lines are the diagonals, or oblique lines connecting the corner angles, and the lines connecting the center of each side.

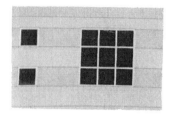

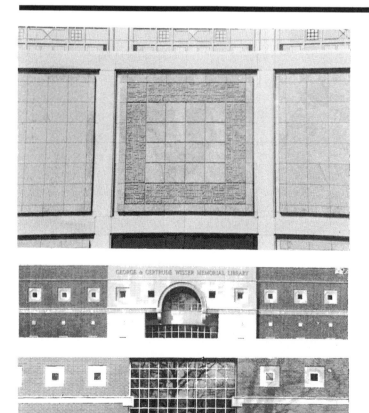

Square

The square is the simplest form in which bi-symmetrical arrange-ments can be found. The most well known is the cross. The square inscribed within a circle and a square circumscribing the circle, indicates the strong affinity between these two geometric forms.

Stepped

Stepped forms are increased or decreased by a series of successive increments, or modulated by incremental stages or steps.

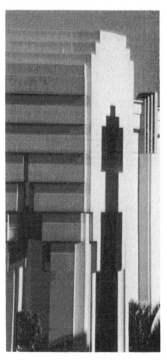

Stepped

Streetscape

This is a diminutive version of the cityscape, relating elements on the ground plane to the viewer. Some of the elements consist of building setbacks, trees, parks and open areas, street furniture and signage. Some are haphazard, others intentionally controlled, yet they all provide the form of our environment.

Suspended

Suspended forms are hung so as to allow free movement, and appear to be supported without attachment to objects below. A suspended roof is one whose load is carried by a number of cables which are under tension, from columns or posts that are in compression which transmit the loads to the ground.

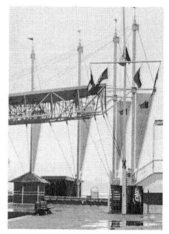

Tensile Structures

Tensile stresses are those that stretch or extend a member or other ductile material, such as a fabric or a membrane. Some forms express this quality even if the material is not fabric, such as concrete shells or slabs.

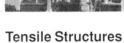

Trapezoidal

A trapezoid is a four-sided figure with unequal sides. The parallel trapezoid has two unequal parallel sides, and two equal nonparallel sides. The symmetrical trapezoid has two pairs of adjacent equal sides.

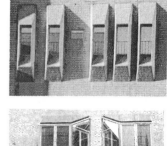

Triangular

The triangle is a plane geometrical figure with three sides and three angles. The equilateral triangle has both equal sides and equal angles. The triangle is one of the most commonly used geometric shapes.

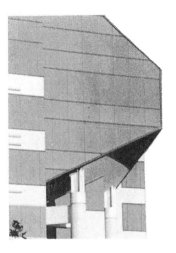

Truncated
    Truncated forms have been cut off at one end, usually the apex, often with a plane parallel to the base.

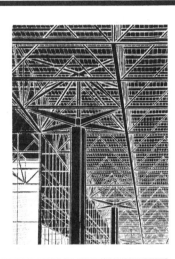

Trussed
    Some facades involve decorative forms derived from trusses that support the structure either horizontally or vertically. These trusses feature triangular patterns, or diagonal bracing which is expressed in the exterior materials, either subtly or boldly.

Wavy

Wavy forms are those that are arranged into curls or undulations, or any graphic representation of curved shapes, outlines or patterns that resembles such a wave.

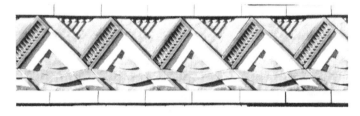

Zigzag

A zigzag is a line formed by angles that alternately project and retreat. It is one of the oldest and most persistent forms. Many moldings have this characteristic, and they are often mixed with other bands of ornament. Zigzags occur on columns, in bands and in larger patterns on cornices.